The Stettner Way

The Life and Climbs of Joe and Paul Stettner

*For Patsi,
My dear friend from
long, long ago.
Hope you enjoy it.
JACK*

John D. Gorby

Colorado Mountain Club Press
Golden, Colorado

Published by The Colorado Mountain Club Press.
Founded in 1912, the Colorado Mountain Club is the
largest outdoor recreation, education and conservation
organization in the Rocky Mountains. Look for our books
at your favorite book seller or contact us at:
710 10th Street, Suite 200, Golden, CO 80401
(303) 996-2743   1 (800) 633-4417
email: cmcpress@cmc.org
website: www.cmc.org

Managing editor: Terry Root.
Graphic design: Terry Root and Steve Meyers.
Proofing: Joyce Carson and Linda Grey.
Original artwork: Jon MacManus (jonsart@realwest.com).
Front cover photo: Joe Stettner in Rocky Mountain
National Park, Colorado in 1942 during filming
of climbing sequences for Fox Movietone News.
Back cover and facing page photo: Joe Stettner
on the first ascent of Stettner Ledges in 1927.
All photographs in The Stettner Way
are courtesy of the family of Joe
and Paul Stettner, except as credited.

The Stettner Way
by John D. Gorby
First Edition
Copyright 2003 by John D. Gorby
Library of Congress Control Number: 2003100609
ISBN Number: 0-9724413-0-1

Manufactured in The United States.
Published in Golden, Colorado.
This publication was made possible by the generous
support of The Mountaineering Foundation of Chicago.

We gratefully acknowledge the
financial support of the people of
Colorado through the Scientific and
Cultural Facilities District of greater
metropolitan Denver, Colorado for
our publishing activities.

SCFD
Scientific & Cultural
Facilities District
Making It Possible.

to young climbers in search of a
role model and a healthy
"approach" to their beloved sport
and
to my wife Laurie, my mother Lois
and my sister Barb, and to the
memory of Joe's wife,
and my friend, Edith.

Acknowledgments

This story is truly the work of many. Several, though, deserve special mention. Jack Fralick, in addition to being the source of many stories, was also a very demanding editor. He tolerated no historical sloppiness on my part and had a bank trustee's eye for detail, a quality I unfortunately lack. Judy Giannetto-Adams, former Editor-in-Chief of the *John Marshall Law School Magazine*, edited my "finished" prose, found much to be done and made many, many suggestions, nearly all of which I have adopted. I truly appreciate her work. I made several friends, Kent Lemmon, Bob Batterman and Peggy Donahue, read, and listen to me read, early drafts; and several other friends, George Pokorny, Jim Pearre and Mike Wilson, read later versions. Their thoughts and encouragement were great. Joe's daughter, Ginnie Madsen, and Paul's wife, Anne Stettner, read through these materials and made valuable suggestions. Both Ginnie and Anne treated me wonderfully during visits to their homes in Laramie and Steamboat Springs. I thank them and the Chicago Mountaineering Club for its prodding and invaluable support. And, of course, I thank my wife Laurie. She suffered through every draft and unrelenting discussion about various issues. She gave me great moral support, as well as important and critical suggestions for improvement.

Writers often say, "I couldn't have done it without these people." I express this sentiment now, feeling that these words have never been more sincerely and accurately used.

(left) Joe on Longs Peak in 1942.

(facing page) Paul on Lone Eagle peak in 1933.

Table of Contents

Foreword

by Jim Detterline
Longs Peak Climbing Ranger
January 2003

In 1986, I was a rookie Longs Peak climbing ranger under the direct supervision of the legendary Billy Westbay. Billy, a famous climber in his own right who had participated in the first one-day ascent of Yosemite Valley's El Capitan, had a great perspective on the climbing history and relevance of the most esthetic routes on Longs Peak. He challenged us with his personal list of great routes to familiarize ourselves with the peak. One of the climbs near the top of his list was the Stettner Ledges.

I was a cocky, young climber then, leading 5.11s and constantly pushing my envelope. The Stettner Ledges had been first ascended in 1927, so I thought that it couldn't be that much of a challenge for me. However, it nearly kicked my butt!

I climbed the route for the first time with Kurt Oliver, the Wild Basin subdistrict ranger who was supervisor to both Billy and myself. Kurt was a world-class backcountry skier, who was also an avid climber. He and I attacked the scenic dihedral system with vigor, but found ourselves humbled by the steep angle, stark holds, clean rock, difficult moves and sustained climbing. In particular, "Paul's Crux," halfway up the climb, was so difficult that I though I was going to fall off of it. This part of the climb was so full of previously-fixed pitons that climbers had nicknamed it "the piton ladder." Indeed, many climbers had resorted to the direct-aid method of pulling up from placement to placement, instead of just using the more common free-climbing method of using pitons simply as protection against a potential fall. Interestingly, most of these pitons were quite new, contrary to generally accepted climbing ethic that you don't add any permanent protection to someone else's first ascent. Just who were these brothers Stettner, who had climbed this intimidating line way back in the prehistoric climbing days of the 1920s, tied into a horse rope, with only a handful of pitons and carabiners for protection?

I got my answer in 1991, when Paul Stettner returned to Estes Park to participate in the first *Longs Peak Reunion,* a festival of climbers and admirers of this inspiring great peak. Paul was invited as a special lecturer to present a talk on his first ascent of the Stettner Ledges. Now an old man in his late eighties, he strode up to the podium with the erect posture and springy gait of a teenager. A legend had returned!

He spoke to us in a clear, strong voice — a humble yet charismatic leader for generations of American climbers. Paul addressed a packed hall of fellow climbers and admirers, regaling us with his tales of the Stettner Ledges and other Colorado adventures. He illustrated his talk with slides reproduced from the black and white prints that he and Joe had made using a large box camera with glass plates, that they had somehow hauled up the face with them. He offered greetings from brother Joe, who was unable to attend from Chicago with his ailing wife, and introduced us to his lovely Anne, and to his son Paul Jr. As Paul shared tales of Anne's and Paul Jr.'s adventures, we came to realize that the Stettners were truly America's First Family of climbers. (Anne was the first woman to climb the East Face of Longs Peak after the horrible Agnes Vaille tragedy in 1925.)

A sizeable number of the gathering's participants were inspired to climb or re-climb the route after Paul's talk. I returned to the climb with Everest noteable, and former ranger, Dr. Tom Hornbein. We pictured the Stettners, gracefully ascending the line with their primitive gear, yet marveled at how difficult, even by modern standards, the route was. There was no doubt why the Stettner Ledges had remained the most difficult climb in North America for twenty years after its first ascent.

Joe Stettner returned to Longs Peak in 1995. The bulk of the stately mountain smiled upon him through the picture window of the Aspen Lodge where he addressed a special gathering of climbers at a luncheon in his honor. He told us about the first ascent and how the Hornsby Direct, a line that was assumed to be a later, straighter finish to the Stettner Ledges, was actually part of the first ascent. The reason that Hornsby's party did not find any Stettner pitons on this route, thus causing them to assume that the line had not been previously climbed, was because the single piton placed by the brothers had fallen out as the leader was climbing!

Paul and Joe passed away in their nineties, untimely demises of those whose hearts were yet so young. I enjoyed getting to know them through conversation, dinners, communications and visits to Steamboat Springs and Devils Lake. They inspired my climbing style, spirit and appreciation for those who had ascended the walls before my generation appeared. They inspired countless numbers of other climbers through their teachings with the Chicago Mountaineering Club, and through their sensitive relationships with family and friends.

The Stettner legend, however, remains intact. Climbers are still humbled by the challenges of the Stettner Ledges and other great Stettner routes. Many aspirants still back off of the difficult Stettner routes, especially the Ledges. And I couldn't begin to count the number of rescues that have occurred to less-gifted parties on these rotues. Perhaps a greater sense of history might have propelled some of these parties to greater success.

That sense of history that connects us to the Stettner brothers is best presented by Jack Gorby. Jack knew and climbed with the Stettners. Within these pages are the clearest firsthand account and the finest of unpublished Stettner photographs. Now you can read the true story of the legendary Stettner brothers, and become inspired to do greater things in life.

*Longs Peak in the Colorado Rockies, the scene of many of the Stettner brothers'
greatest adventures and a pivotal place in the history of American mountaineering.
(Courtesy Colorado Mountain Club)*

Preface

W hat a privilege it must be to achieve fame and high regard in the area of one's youthful passion, and to live long enough to put it all into a thoughtful and wise perspective. Most of us experience neither fame nor long life. A few, one or the other. Although the combination is surely not unique, it is unusual. The rest of us can, and ought, to take advantage and learn from the wisdom and insight this rare combination brings. Thus the motivation to write this story. It is a book about a climber and mountaineer, Joe Stettner, and his brother Paul. Within the early American mountaineering community, the Stettner name became legendary. And so, on one level, *The Stettner Way* is about two mountaineering legends, full of boldness, adventure, excitement and big emotions. On another level, I hope it is about life, and about what is important, gained from the perspective of an old and dignified gentleman with much to be proud of, and much to offer.

Originally I entitled this story "Joe's Solo," which seemed to have a poetic ring. "Joe's Solo" comes from a very controversial solo climb that Joe Stettner did on the East Face of Longs Peak, and that reflects Joe's attitude toward climbing and life, as I hope the reader will soon understand. But "Joe's Solo" is misleading because Joe's story is also his brother Paul's story.

Joe and Paul shared a dream and lived it together, challenging themselves on intimidating rock walls and mountain faces, and exploring their beloved mountains for the sheer joy it brought them. They shared ideals, and were apparently unmoved and unconcerned by the thoughts and views of others. Climbing was their form of artistic expression, which only in later years, were they willing to share with others. Most of their great climbs were done together.

Thus, the story of the one is the story of the other. As a friend put it, "they were inseparable." They were deeply devoted brothers and climbing partners, circumstances designed to create the closest of bonds between two persons. This bond was forged by the tragic circumstances of their childhood and constantly strengthened by the mountains. "Joe's Solo" did not do justice to this partnership.

I wish very much that this were equally Paul's story. To the extent this has been possible, I have tried to make it so. But circumstances are so powerful, and in the end determine the nature of things, including the nature of this story. I came to see the Stettners' climbing adventures through Joe's eyes. Although Joe and Paul lived in Chicago for many years, Paul had moved to Steamboat Springs, Colorado before I arrived in the Windy City. Due to this happenstance, I became acquainted with Joe, not Paul, and over the years Joe and I became friends, a friendship that became of ever increasing importance to me and, I believe, to him. As a consequence, the story is primarily Joe's, albeit through my lens of admiration, respect and love. It is the only story I know and the only one I can tell. And it reflects Joe's philosophy of climbing and life. In this sense only, "Joe's Solo" was not a bad title.

Jack Fralick, who plays prominently in this story, wrote a short piece about Joe and Paul on the 50th anniversary of their climb of the Ledges and entitled it "The Stettner Way."[1] After fretting about an appropriate title throughout the writing of this story, I got the idea that Fralick had captured the spirit of it all with this title. So, with his blessing, I have confiscated his title.

My admiration for Joe and Paul Stettner is shared by all members of the Chicago Mountaineering Club (CMC) to which they belonged. Some of the older members climbed with them and have glowing first hand stories to tell. Younger members have only heard of their mountaineering feats, but re-tell them with awe. The Settners were true mountaineering greats, not just good Midwestern rock climbers. We all seemed to understand that they climbed for the love of it. Importantly for us flatlanders, they gave the whole club a sense of credibility as climbers.

Joe was about 70 when I became involved with the Chicago Mountaineering Club. So, we never climbed together. But I must have displayed much enthusiasm for climbing, and Joe and his wife, Edith, took a friendly and supportive interest in me and my mountaineering ambitions. And so it was climbing that we had in common, and it was our shared passion for climbing that formed the basis of our friendship. During this period, it was Joe's climbs that fascinated me: Stettner Ledges, Lone Eagle Peak, East Face of Monitor, North Ridge of the Grand Teton and on and on. And I loved his stories.

During the early 1980s several prominent members of the Chicago Mountaineering Club began urging me to write about the Stettner brothers. They apparently knew of our close relationship and felt I had a duty to do the writing. I resisted, mainly because I had other commitments, and because I did not know what to say.

Others who have written about the Stettner brothers were primarily interested in their climbs. I didn't know what I could add. But as our friendship grew, and I got to know Joe and Edith better and better, Joe began to tell me about other aspects of his life. I learned about another side of Joe, one that is equally fascinating and worthy of high regard. I had begun to see

Joe in a new and very different light; not just as a climber of great boldness, skill and courage, but as an earnest and admirable human being. This, perhaps more than the climbing, motivated me to attempt to tell this story. Edith's death gave me the final push. It was a very emotional time for me. I wanted to help Joe, but didn't know what to do. It was at that time that I got a sense of the story I wanted to tell. I also sensed that Joe needed to tell his story as well. As it turned out, we had a year and a half to do it.

Most of this story is based on over 20 years of conversations and discussions with Joe, and his occasional writings. As much as possible, I have tried to tell the story with Joe's own words. A portion is based on the work of others; including Paul, who wrote a couple of short passages about the climbs, Jack Fralick, a founder of the Chicago Mountaineering Club and the brother's climbing partner and friend, Jim Peavler, who worked on a Stettner biography, Marvin David, who interviewed Joe on articles in magazines, CMC newsletters, and chapters in climbing books, and on tales that older CMC members have shared with me. In short, this is the work of many.

Out of curiosity, admiration and a longing for grand adventure, I have climbed many of the Stettner routes. I took a number of photographs on these climbs and intended to use them here, but soon concluded that Joe and Paul's are so much better suited for this book. They took many, starting with their early years in Germany. Thus, Joe and Paul are the source of most of the photographs in this book.

I wish to add a thought about the Stettner climbs. Today climbers have very sophisticated equipment and clothing; fancy, light and easily removable camming and wedging devices, long, light and nearly unbreakable ropes to protect climbs, shoes that stick amazingly well on rock and enable even the oafish to feel like a climber, and light weight, warm and waterproof clothing. And, of course, the techniques of climbing have improved significantly. Joe and Paul, equipped with heavy wool clothing, felt soles on their rock shoes, a few pitons and a short one-half inch hemp rope, had none of these advantages. My more modern-day efforts on their routes have only increased my awe and admiration. These were true mountaineers. It is with these feelings about the Stettners that I attempt to tell this story.

Finally, as I have listened to Joe's story and thought about it, I have become increasingly aware that Joe and Paul's lives and climbing are, to a large degree, a consequence of momentous world events far beyond their control. In retelling their story, I have felt it important to sketch these historical events in an effort to show the impact on their lives of the close of World War I and the beginning of the Hitler era and World War II — all intimately related events. I know of no other way of understanding Joe and Paul, and telling their story.

chapter 1

Joe at 94

"**E**dith ist nicht mehr."[2] With these simple words Joe Stettner received me in the living room of his modest, 1920-style bungalow in a working-class neighborhood on the northwest side of Chicago. The living room was typical middle class, with the exception of the remarkable hammered copper reliefs *(repoussé)* that adorned the entry way and walls. The largest of these depicted the Chicago skyline. Other scenes suggested the mountains, capturing in copper impression the Edelweiss of Stettner's native Alps and the Bighorn Sheep of America's Rocky Mountains. These are the work of Joe Stettner — coppersmith and artist, climber and mountaineer.

I held his hand, and we walked into the adjacent dining room, which was occupied primarily by a large table with an exquisitely detailed lace table cloth upon which were several neat piles of letters. A large, black and white photograph of the East Face of Longs Peak, the imposing monarch of the Front Range, hung on the wall, dominating the room much as the peak dominates the northern Colorado Rockies.

Although Joe and I have occasionally spoken German together, it was a surprise to hear him speak in his native tongue now. His beloved Edith was no more, and perhaps to express his deep-felt sorrow, his words came out in his native language. I wondered how the old man could sustain such a blow as this. For some time I had felt that it would be better for Joe to go first.

"Let's go out for dinner," I suggested, "to your favorite restaurant."

"I haven't been out since Edith died. I don't know if I can," was his reply. We went anyway to the Blue Angel, a modest, long-established restaurant near Foster and Milwaukee Avenues, several blocks from Joe's home.

He was then a very old man, slight, frail and in obvious pain from a backache. He walked unsteadily, but managed with a cane. He wore an old, cream-colored turtleneck sweater, suspenders and a worn, slightly torn blue coat. During dinner, he struggled a little with his knife as he tried to cut a piece of butt steak. "I should have ordered fish," he said as he sipped from his glass of Chablis. It was hard to believe he was 94 years old.

There were clear traces of an earlier time — his hair was still dark, his eyes still gleamed and his humor still flashed. And yet he was also suffering from two great losses. In 1994 he lost Paul, his brother, kindred soul and life-time climbing partner; in August 1995, he lost Edith, his dearest friend, constant companion and wife of 52 years. His mind was on Edith and his loss, as we sat together at the Blue Angel.

"Don't cry on me, Joe," the waitress said as she hovered over him with obvious affection. "Joe and Edith have been coming here for years," she explained. "And this loss of Edith is so hard on him."

The scene seemed somewhat incongruous to me. The man sitting across the table was frail, emotional, vulnerable and deeply grieving. Yet, there sat Joe Stettner, one of the greats of American mountaineering history. He and his brother Paul are icons of daring amongst climbers. Their names brings great and bold climbs to mind — Stettner Ledges of the East Face of Longs Peak, considered to have been Colorado's, if not America's, most difficult climb for two decades, Stettner Couloir on the Grand Teton, Stettner Rocks and Stettner Overhang at Devils Lake, to list several of the climbs and mountain places named after them. There are more. Ask any climber familiar with American climbing history. They know about the Stettners — strong, bold, ice-water running through their veins. But the legend does not tell the story of the man. I had become aware of this some time ago.

"Joe," I said, "we've been friends for a long time, and you've often told me about your climbs and your life. For some time, several people have encouraged me to write about the climbs that you and Paul made together. I've hesitated. But now I want to do it. What do you think?"

"If you want to do it, I'm willing to help you," he replied. "Please come back next Thursday morning." I was pleased with his response and impressed that, in the midst of his grief, he was willing to take on an endeavor that would inevitably bring back painful memories.

The following Thursday I arrived at his doorstep. And our task began.

childhood and Youth

C hicago was cold and icy during the first weeks of December 1995, but Joe's house, as always, was warm and comfortable. Joe settled in the recliner chair in his living room. "Now we can begin our story," he announced. "I'll start from the beginning.

"I was born on September 8, 1901. Soon I'll be 95. My brother Paul was born nearly five years later on July 15, 1906. We were the fourth and fifth of six children born to Joseph Stettner Sr., and his wife Leokadia Brandl. Our home was the Bavarian city of Munich, located about 30 miles north of the German Alps.

"My father had a good trade. He was an excellent wood engraver and made woodcuts for printing. He used cherry for his woodcuts because it is so finely grained that, when polished and finished, it is like polished metal. He was very proud of his work. It was a highly paid job in the industry. He made more money than others in his trade but not enough to support our big family, because we came along one after another. There were six of us kids in the family — three boys and three girls. I was the fourth. Because of the size of our family, we were very poor. Often we didn't have enough money for shoes. Sometimes it seemed, we didn't have enough food to eat.

"In those days, there were no cars. Hardly anyone had them. On the streets you could see horses and wagons making deliveries of milk, ice, vegetables, all sorts of things, to homes.

"The Isar River ran through the heart of Munich. There also

The Stettner family in 1907. Joe, at age 5, is seated to the left
of his mother and 4 year-old Paul is held by Joseph Sr.

were several side streams. Water was tapped from them to power factory machinery. Canals were dug and the water was channeled to water wheels that powered a main drive shaft, and then to other shafts connected to the machinery. No electricity. No turbines. It was a direct connection from power to power.

"You ask about childhood. And you know, it's funny what stays in your mind. I can remember when I was about four years old — maybe even younger, perhaps three. I was playing in a sandbox with a little bucket and a shovel when some kid came along. He was much bigger than I, and he took my bucket. So I said, 'This is my bucket, give it to me.' And he said, 'Go away, it's mine now.' Well, I didn't think so, so I took my shovel and hit him right in the face. He started to bleed. Maybe he only had a little scratch, but I felt like, '*Oh!* Maybe I killed him.' I felt sorry. Anyway I got my bucket back.

"I also remember my first climb. It was at about the same time as the bucket incident. I was three or four. There was a stone fountain that was about six feet high. Well, I wasn't a monkey, but I decided to climb it. I made the climb pretty well, but right below the summit I fell down, hit my head and was knocked out. I was bleeding, worse than the kid who took my bucket! They had to carry me home. It was my first climb. And I fell.

"By the age of nine or ten, I had a new beginning for my climbing experiences. I remember that I was never afraid of heights or exposure. Many times I tried to catch canary birds that had escaped from homes in our neighborhood. Some of us kids would stand on windowsills of the third or fourth floor of buildings in an effort to catch these birds. We climbed up on the stone buildings and drain pipes, and never thought anything of it. It seems that we never fell, nor broke any bones.

"Our family was pretty poor. We could always use an extra buck. My father knew a photographer in Munich who was looking for some models for postcards, advertising life in Bavaria. He told my father, 'You've got some cute kids there, how about some of them posing for me?' My father said 'OK,' because he could make a little money out of it. I was six years old at the time. This photographer used me and my sister, posing in traditional costume, doing all kinds of things. In one photograph, I was sticking my head out of a beer barrel with a herring in my hand, a bottle of seltzer water in front of me and a sign that said: *Seltzer water and herring is the best remedy for hangovers.* Another one showed a bunch of us holding up beer steins with a letter on each one that, all together, spelled **PROSIT**. I held the stein with the letter 'P'.

Joe appeared in these postcards made in 1906 and which were sold for many years afterwards. In the left photo, he is sticking his head out of the barrel, and he is on the far left of the bottom photo.

"Then, many years later, after Hitler was defeated in World War II, my mother went on a hike with some friends along the river outside Munich. It was a nice fall day in 1948. They stopped at a kiosk for some refreshments and there on the counter was that postcard with me holding the beer stein when I was six years old. This was 41 years later. My mother mailed it to me. She wrote on it, 'Look, you're famous. They're still selling your picture.' Imagine that. After two wars, Germany was destroyed, but they were still selling that postcard. I still have the postcard. In fact, I have both of them.

"On the street, we all played Indians a lot, with feathers and everything. We saw pictures of Indians in books, and it looked like a good part to play. Of course, we had to have bows and arrows. These weren't things you could buy — not that we had any money anyhow. So we made them ourselves. To make a bow, we'd take the ribs from an old umbrella, bend them and tie them tight with a string. Then we had to have some arrows, so we went out and got some small branches from a willow tree. By 1914, when I was already 13 years old, World War I started. So, of course, we didn't play Indians any more. We played soldiers instead. We did this in spite of my father's feelings about the war.

"At the outbreak of the First World War, my father was encouraged to become an officer and fight for the Fatherland. He said, 'No, they must draft me.' They said to him, 'Do you want to live forever? Go! Fight!' My father responded, 'Fight for whom? Why should I die for the Kaiser's cause.' Later, right after the war, my mother put up a flag. My father said, 'Take that flag down. Do you know how many people died for the Kaiser? Take it down.' That was my father. I think it was his anti-war sentiments that first brought him into contact with Kurt Eisner, who became prime minister of Bavaria.

"My father was a leader in his union. He felt strongly about improving the situation of workers. He was a union representative at many meetings in Germany and throughout Europe. It was a good job for him because he was not afraid to speak out.

"My father was also a very active member of the Bavarian Independent Socialist Party of Kurt Eisner, and developed a personal and political friendship with him. They were quite close. I went to a number of meetings with my father, met Kurt Eisner and often heard him speak. He was Jewish and an intellectual, but he was different from other intellectuals. Although I was young, maybe 17, I remember him as having a big white beard. I also was impressed by his strength.

"My father also knew Ernst Toller, who was a poet and an important person in the Independent Socialist Party. He was also acquainted with Rosa Luxemburg from Berlin and talked about her at home. For a while, my father was the president of a section of the Independent Socialists. That says something about his involvement in politics. He never held an official government office. He also was never a communist.

"I wasn't very interested in politics, but it was an important topic in our home. My mother called my father a 'radical revolutionary.'

"My mother and father were Catholics. Our family didn't practice very much. My mother sneaked out to church and my father didn't try to stop her from going. He believed that, 'You do something, not pray about it.'

"I was 14 years old before I got to the mountains. Before that, my mother would take us for long hikes to visit relatives. Most Saturdays or Sundays, when my father would go fishing, my mother would take a bunch of us for hikes of about ten kilometers through the woods. It was all uphill. In the lower sections, there would be willows and so on, but as you climbed it was all pine forest. Still higher, you had the smaller trees — the larches. All up hill. That's how I got my climbing legs — from my mother.

"She was in good shape and liked to walk. My mother was a good cook and housewife. When we were naughty, she would beat us up with a wooden spoon. When she would go after one of us kids, the others would defend. So she would hit the others. Eventually when I was 18 or 19, she came after me with that spoon when I was kidding her. I grabbed her arms and said, 'No more of that.'

"My brother Max, who was five years older than me, was a fisherman like my father. Max and my father spent a lot of time together fishing, while the rest of us went hiking with our mother. Later, fishing became Max's main activity. I didn't like to fish. It was too quiet. There is no movement. I couldn't just sit there waiting for the fish to bite. I had to move.

"When I was 14, my father decided it was time I learned a trade. I had no idea what I wanted to do, and my father didn't think I had any real talent to follow in his footsteps. He thought I was just a common man. He saw my weak point. He thought I wasn't college material, so he made connections with a fellow who worked as a bookkeeper in a shop where they did copper and sheet metal work. My father said, 'I don't know what I'm going to do with my son. He's good with his hands, and he wants to learn something.' The guy agreed to talk to the owner of the shop. It was a small place, with only about 15 or 20 employees. Later, I developed into a very skilled craftsman with metal. I wish my father had lived to see what I've done, to see some of my art work.

"I was hired as an apprentice for three-and-a-half years. I worked

Joe (at right), age 15, while apprenticed to a coppersmith.

six days a week — five full days, and on Saturday I'd work a half day and then clean up the shop, clean the tools, and so on. I was paid two *marks* a week. That's a dollar.

"Throughout my apprenticeship as a coppersmith and sheet metal worker, I often was called upon to work on the roof tops of high buildings. The heights never bothered me. I remember once that my boss sent me out with an older man to a tower with a flagpole on top of it. The rope on top of the flagpole had come out. We were supposed to replace it with a new rope. The older man told me to climb up and replace it. I don't remember if he put a waistline on me or not. If he did, I don't remember it. I didn't think anything of it. It was child's play for me. I was about 15 or 16 years old at the time. In 1962, when I returned to Munich, I walked by that tower. It was the Isartor Tower on the Isar River. And I thought, 'How easy it has been for me to be in exposed places all my life.'

"My father also found an apprenticeship for Paul as a photoengraver, my father's craft. Paul then became the one to follow in his footsteps. He also became a member of my father's union.

"That's a small picture of my life before the end of the war."

chapter 3

A Family Tragedy

I returned to Joe's house two days later. He was anxious about packing everything up for an impending move to Laramie, Wyoming, to be close to his daughter Ginni. "How am I ever going to deal with all these things, all these books?" he complained. He had planned to give his mountaineering materials to the Chicago Mountaineering Club and to the American Alpine Club.

I, though, wanted to learn more about Joe's life at the end of World War I and about the beginning of his climbing career, before he and his brother emigrated. Joe finally settled down and continued his story.

"The political situation at the end of the First World War was confusing, chaotic and awful. It destroyed German society, and eventually had a devastating impact on our family, on Paul, and on me. I'm not a historian and do not know or cannot remember a lot of what happened. It was such a long time ago, and I was quite young. All I can do is add some of my own memories and impressions. In some ways, they are different from what the history books say."

Toward the end of the war in the late summer of 1918, when Joe was 16 and Paul 12, the German High Military Command, concerned with their worsening military situation, demanded that the government seek an armistice and urged the formation of a new government that would impress the Allied Forces with its representative and liberal character. The generals hoped these changes would enable the old regime to maintain as much power and control as possible. The government accepted this advice and began armistice negotiations.

The Allied Forces, however, insisted that Germany rid itself of its princes as a condition to an armistice. The Kaiser, William II, wanted no part of this. In spite of governmental efforts to persuade him to abdicate, the Kaiser struggled to keep his throne and recapture his power. He fantasized about mobilizing his armies and marching to Berlin to regain control. These problems seriously delayed an armistice and a tolerable peace.

News that the government was seeking an armistice leaked out and had a far reaching and shattering effect on major factions of German society — on the supporters of the war who were now devastated, on the workers and peasants who had suffered during the war and now lost their sense of restraint, and on members of the armed forces who now lost their discipline. It also had a major effect on the extreme Left, which yearned for a truly revolutionary change in the German social structure and sensed that the time for revolution had come.

In the meantime, German admirals, fearing that the government would surrender their navy to the British Fleet, ordered their ships to set sail and engage the British in the North Sea. Large groups of sailors disobeyed these orders and mutinied. Although the immediate crisis was resolved, an apparent sailors' victory encouraged widespread resistance to military orders throughout northern Germany and brought about general and public demands for the government to strike an immediate peace with the Allied Forces and for the Kaiser to abdicate. Even more unsettling for the government was the fact that sailors took over garrisons in several northern German cities. The government feared it had lost control.

This set the stage for dramatic events in the Stettners' home city of Munich. The Hapsburg Empire of Austria-Hungry had recently collapsed, making Bavaria vulnerable to invasion from the south — a threat that caused the utmost fear in Munich, as well as in the German capital of Berlin. The fear of a harsh treaty of surrender aggravated the situation even more. It was this political environment that thrust Kurt Eisner, left-wing socialist, political associate and friend of Joseph Stettner Sr., into power.

Eisner was a remarkable character. Charles Flood[3] described him as a birdlike little man, complete with a Berlin accent and the Jewish religion, long wispy gray beard, big black hat, thick steel-rimmed glasses and seedy suits. He was an intellectual, student of Kant and Nietsche, drama critic, satirical journalist and a Berliner, who at the turn of the century, landed in prison for nine months as punishment for ridiculing the Kaiser.

At 40 years of age, Eisner left Berlin for Munich, where he became political editor of the Social Democrat's *Muenchener Post*. Although he urged political reforms, the Social Democrats regarded him more as a bohemian than a person with sufficient leadership ability to win over Bavaria's Catholic working men. It was assumed by both the Left and the Right that the support of the working classes was the key to gaining and maintaining political power in Germany. Thus, the Social Democrats did not believe Eisner had any real political potential.

Later, Eisner took an early opposition to the war, a position that collided with wartime military press censorship. He lost his job, which thrust him into poverty but provided ample time to change from political critic to political activist. It was during this time that he met Joseph Stettner Sr., who shared his beliefs about the war and was a member of the Catholic worker class. Joe's father was the kind of person Eisner needed to further his political ambitions.

In 1917, Eisner founded the Bavarian branch of the Independent Socialists and organized a strike for peace, an activity that earned him another eight-month prison term, as well as a reputation as an anti-war activist and martyr.

On November 7, 1918, soon after his release from prison, Eisner appeared on the Theresian Meadow, the site of the Oktoberfest, before a huge crowd intent on listening to the speeches of socialist leaders. Eisner captured the day by demanding that Bavaria and Austria join together and proclaim peace in the name of Germany, since Berlin "had neither the will nor power . . . to reach an immediate peace."[4] Then Eisner shouted, "Scatter throughout the city, occupy barracks, seize weapons and ammunition, win over the rest of the troops, and make yourselves masters of the government."[5]

The crowd obeyed, and Eisner led his followers to the barracks and garrisons where they seized arms. By evening, they controlled all military headquarters in Munich. Before midnight, the city was covered with posters announcing a new government — the Bavarian Republic. The next day, Eisner set up a cabinet, naming himself prime minister and foreign minister, and set out to establish a peace for Bavaria that would protect it from an Allied invasion from the south and from an unfair peace or worse.

The significance of the events of November 7 and 8, 1918, that took place in Munich, cannot be underestimated. They brought matters to a rapid and dramatic conclusion in the German capital of Berlin. The government concluded that it had lost control of Germany. A day later, on November 9th, the Reichs Chancellor announced the resignation of his government and the abdication of the Kaiser and the Crown Prince.

He also announced that Frederick Ebert, the head of the Social Democratic Party, and in sentiment a monarchist, would become Chancellor. He would call a constitutional assembly to determine the form of the new state.

The German Republic was proclaimed. Later that evening, Kaiser William II fled across the German border into Holland, thereby bringing an end to the dynasty of Hollenzollern monarchs that had ruled Germany for 500 years. Two days later, on November 11, 1918, the armistice was concluded.

The new Chancellor Ebert tried without success to regain control of northern Germany and Munich, and to retain a semblance of the old order. But soldiers, worker's councils, the Independent Socialists — with whom Joseph Stettner Sr. was affiliated — and the Spartacus Union (soon to become the German Communist Party) challenged the legitimacy of Ebert's government. This frustrated the efforts of the government even more.

The Spartacus Union constituted a particularly serious threat. It had two outstanding leaders, Karl Liebknecht and the Polish revolutionary Rosa Luxemburg, with whom Joe's father was acquainted. They both perceived Chancellor Ebert as a true enemy of the revolution. They were likely correct, for Ebert was determined that the Bolshevik Revolution of Russia would not be repeated in Germany. In short, it was a time of high stakes, intense political struggle and government frustration over its inability to control the extreme Left.

Confronted with these overwhelming problems, Chancellor Ebert allied his Social Democrats with the Supreme Army Command against the extreme Left (principally the Spartacists and the Independent Socialists of Kurt Eisner) to prevent a Bolshevist-type revolution. In reaction to this, on January 5, 1919, the Spartacists and 200,000 workers surrounded the Reichs Chancellery in Berlin and held the government captive for a short period.

The government tried in vain to quash this revolt with local police. The army having been reduced in numbers because of the armistice was too weak to keep the revolt under control. To supplement these forces, the generals encouraged former officers to recruit volunteer forces to resist Bolshevism and restore law and order. The response to their call for assistance was remarkable. Demobilized officers and soldiers, university students and adventurers, patriots and drifters all responded. The result was the formation of the so-called *Free Corps* — armed groups of roaming soldiers, who were secretly supported by the regular army, and who became the scourge of a new Germany and a hotbed of later Nazism.

On January 10, 1919, the Free Corps launched an attack on Spartacist Headquarters in Berlin and, with flame throwers and artillery supplied by the regular army, soon brought Berlin under control. In the course of the recapture, they killed a number of Spartacists — including Rosa Luxemburg and Karl Liebknecht, who were captured and murdered five days later. The Spartacists sought retaliation, which led to fighting between Independent Socialists and Spartacists on one side, and the Free Corps on the other.

In the meantime, Kurt Eisner's fortunes also suffered. Although not a Bolshevik like Luxemburg and Liebknecht, Eisner was often associated with them and discussed in the same breath. In addition, Eisner failed in his efforts to strike a separate peace with the Allied forces. The Bavaria economy suffered, in part because of his unrealistic welfare policies.

In January 1919, Germany and Bavaria held parliamentary elections. Joe Stettner assisted his father by working for Eisner's Independent Socialists during December 1918 and January 1919. In spite of his efforts, Eisner's party suffered a defeat and lost power. During the weeks that followed, Eisner appealed for socialist unity to build a coalition, but had little success. On his way to announce his resignation on February 21, 1919, Eisner was shot and killed by a young nobleman, and right-wing army officer, named Arco-Valley. Joe believes that this was part of a plot devised by Right-wing university students. An hour later, in retaliation, a member of the Revolutionary Workers Council entered the state parliament building and shot the majority socialist leader.

Joe remembers his father coming home that night and exclaiming, "They shot Kurt Eisner. The whole Bavarian government is corrupt. Now we are going to see some real trouble!"

The political reaction was intense. Bavaria was plunged into anarchy. Extreme Leftists forced priests at gun point to toll church bells for days to mourn Kurt Eisner's death. By April, large groups of workers were calling for revolution. A general strike was held. Tempers were running high, and the dangers were so great that the Bavarian government, that succeeded Eisner's Independent Socialists, decided to move to Bamburg. Taking advantage of the Bavarian government's absence from Munich, the extreme Left attempted to take control of the city and set up a Soviet-style republic. For a short time, this Soviet republic was controlled by a band of tribunes that included Ernst Toller, a dramatist, poet of the Bohemian life and an acquaintance of Joe's father. This government, however, was short lived.

On May 1, 1919, army troops were dispatched from Berlin and Free Corps volunteers entered Munich. They set up road blocks and barricades, moving into the center of the city. Extreme Leftist workers had killed some hostages, and the Free Corps massacred several hundred persons, including non-communists, in retaliation. Soon, they overthrew the communist regime.

During this period, according to Joe, his father was "supervising the police in an effort to prevent looting by the people. Items that had been looted were recovered and kept at the police department. But looters managed to break into the police department and steal the items held there."

"On May 1, 1919, the Free Corps came into the city with the intention of overthrowing the communist government there," Joe recalled. "I remember there was fighting in the streets. Not many people left their homes, but my father wanted to check on something at the place where he worked. So he left the house, carrying a mountain walking stick with a horn grip. It was May 2, 1919.

"Just a half a block from our house, he came upon a roadblock. There were some young guys there, all wearing brown shirts, some with rifles. They were pushing around a one-legged war veteran, kicking the crutches out from under him, laughing and knocking him down. My father couldn't take a thing like this.

"'You lousy kids!' he yelled at them. 'You weren't even dry behind the ears when this guy was fighting for your Fatherland. What do you think you're doing?'

Joseph Stettner Sr.

"They said, 'None of your business!' And they went after him. They fought for a while. I don't know if my father hit them with his walking stick or what. But one of these guys shot him at close range, right in the kidney. My father took the shot, then took out a knife he had with him, lunged at the guy and shouted, 'I'm not going to die alone!' And he stabbed the guy in the chest. Then he fell to the street. And he bled to death.

"After father was killed, they looked at his papers and learned that he was from Kurt Eisner's group.

"I heard all of this from a witness who was there. I didn't see it, but I was a half a block away, and I heard the shot. I didn't know it was my father. And you know, he died right there on the *Gaertnerplatz*, on a spot right next to the beer garden where Hitler, Goering, Goebbels and all that gang would meet to make plans for the Nazi party."

When Joe first told me this story in the late 1980s, he began to cry. "They just killed him," he murmured. Later, when I left his home, I thought, "It's over 65 years ago, and he still feels the pain."

chapter 4

The Call of the Mountains

*A*fter the regular army and the Free Corps gained control of Munich in the spring of 1919, the moderate Social Democratic government was nominally restored for a short period. Real political power, however, had passed to the Right, which, at that time, was composed of the regular army and monarchists. In short, it was a group of conservatives who despised the democratic Republic in Berlin and the Leftists who had earlier controlled Munich.

William Shirer wrote about this period in *The Rise And Fall Of The Third Reich* . As he explains:

> March 14, 1920, the Reichswehr overthrew the Hoffmann Socialist government and installed a right-wing regime under Gustav von Kahr. And now the Bavarian capital became a magnet for all those forces in Germany which were determined to overthrow the Republic, set up an authoritarian regime and repudiate the Diktat of Versailles. Here the condottieri of the free corps, including members of the Ehrhardt Brigade, found a refuge and welcome. Here General Ludendorff settled, along with a host of other disgruntled, discharged Army officers. Here were plotted the political murders, among them that of Matthias Erzberger, the moderate Catholic politician who had the courage to sign the armistice when the generals backed out; and of Walther Rathenau, the brilliant, cultured Foreign Minister, whom the extremists hated for being a Jew and for carrying out the national government's policy of trying to fulfill at least some of the provisions of the Versailles Treaty.

It was in this fertile field in Munich that Adolf Hitler got his start.

The sentences that the Bavarian courts imposed on Leftists and Rightists for their "revolutionary" and treasonous activities give an indication of the atmosphere in Munich at this time. Eugen Levine, chief executive of the short lived Bavarian Soviet Republic, for example, was executed for treason; Ernst Toller, Joseph Stettner Sr.'s associate, received a ten-year prison sentence. Count Arco, who murdered Kurt Eisner, on the other hand received a brief term of fortress imprisonment. The soldier who kicked Bavarian Soviet leader Gustav Landauer to death received only five weeks.

It was in the midst of this volatile and unpredictable world that Joe and Paul found themselves after their father's murder. It was reflected at home and in their emotional state. Joe once remarked, "If they had not killed my father when they did, they would have killed him in a week or two. He was strong minded and would not have backed down. He would not have been able to shut up."

It was reflected at work. "The owner of the shop where I was employed, a Danish guy named Rasmussen, was a real Jew hater. When I returned to work after my father was killed, Rasmussen said to me, 'Don't worry. Your father didn't amount to anything. He was a revolutionary. You're better off.' I felt like killing him. I was only 19 years old. Rasmussen apparently liked me, because he told me that he would help me get another job. But I was so hurt by what he said that I didn't want his help and didn't accept it. Later, when I finished my apprenticeship and I left that job, I told him to 'Go to hell!'

"I then took a new job. But the foreman there was also a Jew hater. It seemed that nearly everyone was. His son became a Nazi and we disliked each other. Nonetheless, we went skiing together. I didn't think that politics should have any place in the mountains and in sports.

"Hatred of Jews and politics became so mixed up and intertwined. Many members of the left-wing were Jewish. The right-wing used this for propagandist purposes. They claimed that the Jews were sympathetic to Russia and to the Bolsheviks. But this was not true.

"As I tell you this story, I feel just like all this was yesterday. In the winter of 1919, a young man from my shop invited me to go skiing. It was about the time I was finished with my apprenticeship. This journeyman, who was about 20 years old, asked me if I liked to ski. I told him that I didn't know and that I had never tried it.

"I told my father about this invitation. He said, 'Why do you want to do that? Save your strength for work and go fishing with me.' I wanted to try skiing, so I went anyway. This was right before my father was killed.

"I had seen skis, because the war was over and they were selling leftover equipment that the mountain troops had used in Russia. It sounded like a good idea, so I got myself a pair of old skis. I don't remember who paid for them. By that time, I was making maybe three or four *marks* a week, but you couldn't buy skis for that. I didn't even have money for the railroad to get there. But this guy took me along anyway.

"They were plain wood skis — ash wood — no edges or anything like that. My boots were regular shoes — army boots — which were clamped by metal side plates on the skis. You wrapped leather straps around them for bindings — nothing fancy.

"We got to the mountain and walked up to a hut, carrying our skis — no ski lifts in those days. It happened that there had been a terrific storm. Trees were blown over and lying all over the slope. Besides that, it was late spring and there wasn't much snow. It was my first time on skis, and all the way up I was saying, 'How the hell do we ever get down?' We stayed in the hut with the wind howling all night, and the next morning, somehow, we got down. And I said, 'You know, that was pretty nice.'

"Once I got the bug, I wanted more. So I asked my brother Paul,

Paul is the young skier in the middle.

who was five years younger than me, if he wanted to go with me. Then my mother, who was in good shape, decided she'd go along too, and take my younger sister. So that was the first Stettner trip. The four of us went up to the mountains and found a hay barn to sleep in.

"Before my father's death, my mother was not very interested in politics. She called him a 'radical revolutionary.' But after his death, she began demonstrating against the right-wing government that was running Bavaria. She became pretty active politically. It took my father's death to wake her up. I said to her one day, 'You're going to get killed just like my father.'

"My older brother Max was also politically involved. He was in the *Heimwehr* or Home Guard, a kind of militia that supported the Republic. Later, the Nazis gained control of the Heimwehr, but at the time, it supported the Republic. Because of his involvement with the Heimwehr, Max had two rifles. When the regular army and the Free Corps took control over Munich, they arrested Max and confiscated his rifles. They also arrested nearly everyone who was associated with the left-wing of the Socialist Party.

"Max, and five or six others, were lined up against a wall to be shot. Several were shot. But a commander there yelled out, 'Stettner! Come here.' Max left the line and went into the commander's office. It turns out that this commander had been a schoolmate of Max's. He kept Max in jail for a while until matters cooled down. Then he let him go. This really frightened Max. After that, Max would have nothing to do with politics. He would only go fishing, something my father loved to do.

"After my father's death, the rest of us continued to hike with my mother. We hiked through the farm lands. Everyone there loved my father. They often said, 'How could they kill him? He was such a good man.' He was only 48 when they killed him. The Independent Socialist Party erected a large grave stone for him. It bears the inscription that my father was a leader in the Independent Socialist Party, and shows two torches pointing upside down. It is still there in Munich.

"During this time, Paul and I started going into the mountains as often as we could. And so we became climbing and skiing partners, and close companions — an association that was not broken until his death.

"At first, we walked the trails, and later we took tours on skis. I remember once we passed a rather steep pinnacle along the trail and noticed a cross on the top. We wondered who could have put it there. We decided that he sure must have been off his rocker. How little did I know at the time that soon Paul and I would be getting *the climbing bug* and start behaving the same way.

"That same summer, Paul and I planned to go to the mountains

The Meiler Hut.

with a group of hikers. A friend of ours, Hanni Arnold, wanted to come along. So we let her join us. She trusted us, and later we took her along on other hard trips. She remained our friend for the rest of her life. For some reason, someone in our group carried along a climbing rope. We went to the Meiler Hut near the Dreitorspitze, which is in the Wetterstein Group. We sat outside the hut and were watching several climbing parties going out to climb the Dreitorspitze. But they all came back and said that they could not make it because of the snow and ice.

"That made Paul and I quite interested. We became anxious to take a stab at it. We took the rope that had been brought along and went out. We made the climb rather easily. Most likely we were so inexperienced that we did not see the danger. We felt strong, and our first taste of success encouraged us further. From then on, we wanted to climb mountains.

"We had heroes. We read and heard about some of the famous mountain climbers like Luis Trenker, Hans Duelfer and others who did some terrific climbs in the Wilde Kaiser Gebirge in Austria. At that time the Wilde Kaiser range was the proving ground for rock climbers. We admired and looked up to these men. Trenker was our biggest hero. He was a great skier and ice climber, and *the* outstanding rock climber in Europe. We read about him and heard about him. My mother gave me a book written by Luis Trenker. It's title is *Meine Berge*. I still have it.

"Trenker and his friends were climbing very hard routes. We didn't think we could do these climbs, so we learned about what they had done earlier and worked on those climbs. Paul and I went out to climb some of these same rocks. We improved step by step. Now, when I compare Trenker's climbs with Stettner Ledges that Paul and I climbed in 1927, I think that we had reached their level of climbing.

The Dreitorspitze (above) and
Paul with Otty Scharnberger
on the summit (right).

"Everytime we planned a big trip to the mountains, we visited the little Alpine Museum in Munich and studied the area on the excellent relief maps they had. We also climbed in a *Klettergarten* in the Isartal near Munich, where climbers practiced. Sometimes we traveled to Kufstein. There, the climbers simply picked a route and climbed it.

"Paul was only 13 or 14 at that time, but he wanted to do everything I could. He had no experience. He was bold, reckless and could climb anything. When you get older and have some brains, you look around and begin to think about what you're doing. You begin to think about what could happen. You begin to think, 'Should I do it or not?' But before that, you don't climb with your brains. You climb with your muscles. That's the way Paul and I were.

"One time, Paul and I decided to climb the Totenkirchl via the

*Paul and friends on
the summit of the
Totenkirchl.*

Zottkamin, Rosserkamin and the Osterweg. We still didn't have our own climbing rope, so Paul borrowed one from a man at his workplace. It took us three hours to get to the top. When we arrived, we were surprised to find the man who loaned Paul the rope sitting on the summit with his partner.

"Paul and I usually went on these trips alone. And we went regularly, so we learned to climb by practice. We'd go out together, without much food or equipment. The little equipment we had was poor, just like we were. We had no sleeping bags or blankets, or anything like that. If the weather was bad, we'd just sleep in a raincoat. And the next morning, we'd start climbing. Often there weren't any trails to the climb. You just went up where you wanted to go.

"In no time, I had become a real smart-aleck. Right away, I thought I was better than anybody else. I didn't need a guide. I didn't need advice. I just saw a mountain and went for it. And Paul always went with me. We were a team. We really taught ourselves how to climb. We stuck our necks out a lot, but we got away with it. The first time we made a tough ascent, we said to each other, 'That wasn't too scary. Not much to it. Well, if that's what it takes to climb a mountain, I guess we're mountain climbers.' And we kept going.

"We had so little money that sometimes we had a hard time just getting to the places we wanted to visit. By 1921 we joined the Neuland Section of the German-Austrian Alpine Club in Munich. This gave us access to the Alpine Club's huts.

"During Christmas time in 1921, Paul and I decided to take a glacier ski tour to the Dresdner Hut in the Stubaier Mountains. The hut is surrounded by glaciers, and we had heard that it was a very nice place. We expected it to be open all year, as were so many of the huts that belonged to the German-Austrian Alpine Club. With that expectation, we took off.

"We took the train from Munich over Innsbruck to Fulpmes and to the end of the railroad line. We loaded ourselves down with skis, ropes, bread and some sausage. We had no blankets or any form of sleeping equipment. Paul was so small — he was only 15, and his pack looked bigger than him!

"From there, we hiked up the valley. In the last significant village before going up into the mountains, we found out that the hut was closed and that no one in the village had the key. Some people in the village wondered what we were doing. 'You kids can't survive up there,' they exclaimed. 'You don't even have blankets.' But there was another little village a bit further on in the mountains, so we continued on, hoping to find someone there with a key. But it was winter and no one stayed there during the winter.

"Because the Dresdner Hut was eight more hours away up a steep hill, and it was late afternoon, we knew we would have to spend the night somewhere without blankets. There was an old barn that was used in the summer for making cheese. It was open and it had a fire pit in the middle of its dirt floor, wooden benches along the walls and a hole in the roof for the smoke to go out. We built a fire, made some tea and tried to stay warm. Soon, the entire barn was filled with smoke, and we started choking. Apparently the hole in the roof did not draw too well. We tried to sleep on the benches, but we were cold and felt like a couple of sausages being cured. To be able to head out in the morning was a relief.

"We decided to continue on to the Dresdner Hut, because we figured that a room had probably been left open for emergencies. For the first mile or so, there was a lot of ice with occasional snow, but nowhere was there enough snow to ski on. We dragged our skis behind us so we wouldn't have to carry them. Everytime we found snow, we tried to ski but the crust was so windblown and icy, and the slope so steep, that we made no progress. Crampons were what we needed, but, of course, we didn't have any. Late in the afternoon, we spotted the hut in the distance.

"Luckily the weather was good. There was little new snow. With renewed energy, we finally reached the hut, only to discover it was locked up tight. Nobody was there and nobody had been there for a long time. It had gotten quite cold and was going to get a lot colder. We simply had to get in. It was impossible for us to stay outside overnight. But everything was closed up. They had even put wooden shutters on all the windows.

"We looked around for a key, but couldn't find one. Then we discovered a shutter that was a little loose. With some effort and prying, we managed to get the shutter open, only to find that there were iron bars over the window. We had heard that the head is thicker than the body and that if the head can get through a narrow space, the rest of the body can follow. I tried to stick my head through the bars, but it didn't go. Because Paul's head was smaller than mine, we decided he should try to squeeze in. I helped Paul squeeze his head between the bars, and then, with my force and his squirming, we got his body through the bars.

"Once he was in, he was supposed to open the door for me. It seemed like ages before he did so. Paul was unable to open the doors from the inside, so he removed the hinges from one of the doors and eventually got the it open. Once inside, we were safe. We made the best of the situation. We found hundreds of blankets to keep us warm and there was a stove with plenty of wood. We eventually got a good fire going and were cozy enough. We stayed for two days and went climbing.

"The weather was spectacular, but the snow — the little of it — was even crustier and icier than the day before. We decided to climb the Schaufelspitze. So, with our ice axes and rope, we set out. But after hours of struggling with ice, rock and inadequate equipment, we decided to give up and return to the hut.

"The next morning, we wrote a note explaining our trespass, left enough money to cover the normal usage fee for the hut and resupplied

The Dresdner Hut, Christmas 1921,

Their failed 1921 attempt on the Schaufelspitze (above) convinced the brothers that they needed to learn about glacier travel techniques.

the wood we had used. We placed all our things outside the hut. While I held the door from the outside, Paul replaced the hinges from the inside, so that the door was closed and locked as before. He then went out through the bars the same way he had come in. We loaded up our gear and started back down the valley.

"When we arrived in the village we had come up through days before, some people came out to talk to us. The rumor was that we had probably died in the cold mountains since we didn't have any real equipment. The villagers said to us, 'You boys must be saints to go up there at this time of year and not get killed.' And I suppose we looked the part.

"Upon our return to Munich, we learned that while we were gone, Max's very religious wife had come home and found that a cross she had placed on the wall had fallen to the floor. This, she believed, was a sure sign that Paul and I had been killed. She was surprised and relieved when we both arrived home unharmed.

"This was one of our first experiences in real mountaineering. I remember it so well. I kept notes at the time, as all German-Austrian Club members were required to do.

"When I was in Munich, I was constantly afraid of being arrested because I was the son of a revolutionary man. It was a problem for all of us. Max, who was five years older, was married, and he had turned his attentions almost totally to his new family. As a result, I took over a big responsibility for my mother and brother and sisters. I guess I was never a teenager. I had to become a man when we lost my father. This was even more true when Max was married. I had to jump from a kid to a man of 55. In so many ways, I had to go out on my own. But I did so with my father's ideas close to my heart.

"In spite of all these problems, or because of them, Paul and I dreamed of more mountaineering trips. Our experiences on the Schaufelspitze persuaded us that we needed to learn more about glacier travel. So, for the next several months, we read about glaciers and traveling on them, and talked to climbers who were willing to tell us about their techniques. Paul and I saved our money and bought some crampons. We continued to spend a lot of hours studying maps in the Alpine Museum. We wanted a great trip that would take us over mountain tops and high valleys. Finally, we decided to do a tour to Grossglockner and Grossvenediger.

"We estimated that this would take us about eight days, and a great deal of the tour would be over glaciers. Our experiences in the mountains were few, and practically none of them involved travel over glaciers. But our study of the relief maps in the museum gave us a good idea of the ups and downs of the tour. Because of our research about glacier techniques, we felt that we had a kind of theoretical knowledge that would get us through.

"Max had a friend five years older than I, who asked if he could join us. He had been in the mountains before and wanted to go again, but needed companions to do so. To our surprise, this older guy had confidence in us.

"I remember our departure date very well. It was my twenty-first birthday — September 8, 1922 — at 5:18 p.m. when we boarded the train for Zell am See in Austria. It was just a few months past Paul's sixteenth birthday. Neither of us looked our age. We had a rope, ice axes, crampons, all the necessary equipment and most of the food we would need to sustain us for eight days. Max's friend brought his own food and equipment. It was 3:45 in the morning when we got off the train. All these details I still have in my record book. At six o'clock in the morning we started our march. First, we hiked on a road for five miles. Then we went up a trail to the Heinrich Schweiger Haus, which is at about 2,900 meters above sea level. We got there early in the afternoon, after a hike of about eight hours.

"Most of the houses and huts in the mountains belonged to the German-Austrian Alpine Club. I recently had become a member of the

"We surely didn't look like experienced mountaineers."
Joe (at right) in 1922 with Peppi Kantner

Section Neuland in Munich, a branch organization. This membership entitled me to use these huts for a reasonable fee. When we arrived at the Schweiger Haus, there were only a few guests. That evening one of the other guests, who had been watching and listening to us, approached me and inquired about our projected tour. Finally, he asked if he could join us.

"We surely didn't look like experienced mountaineers. But then, people are very much discouraged from going on the glaciers alone. This man had his own ice ax and crampons. So we agreed to have him come along.

"The next day we left early. After a short walk on a trail, we reached the glacier. Our plan was to get to the Oberwalder Hut and climb as many peaks as we could on the way. We put on our crampons. Paul and I roped together, and the other fellows roped up behind us. This glacier walk was very impressive, with the high mountains that stood all around us. We stayed high, hardly dropping below the 3,000 meter level all the way. This way, we were able to climb lots of peaks. The first peak we came to was the Grosses Wiesbachhorn, which is 3,564 meters high. We climbed it.

"Nearby were several other peaks — Kloekerin at 3,419 meters,

Bratschenkopf at 3,413 meters and Grosser Baerenkoph at 3,419 meters. We climbed these, too. They were all short climbs. At one place, in a crevassed area, my knapsack string broke and our food rolled down toward a crevasse. Luckily, we were able to save it all. This was the most exciting experience for us during our nine hours to the Oberwalder Hut, which is situated at 2,972 meters.

"The weather was still perfect when we arrived at the hut. We were fascinated by the beautiful view of the circle of mountains around us. Across the Pasterzen Glacier was the Grossglockner, the highest mountain in Austria at 3,798 meters. The Glockerwand is to the right of it. We could spot the Erzherzog Johann Hut on the Adlersruhe, which stands at 3,465 meters, just to the left of the Grossglockner, which was our next day's goal.

"In the morning, after storing most of our food in the hut, since we planned to return the next day, we started our descent of the Pasterzen Glacier to an elevation of about 2,400 meters. We then went up the icefalls to the hut on the Adlersruhe. The weather was still perfect, and we had a good night's rest in the hut.

"Early in the morning we were the first on the summit of Grossglockner. It took us only one-and-a-half hours. With just a few climbers behind us, it was enjoyable to look around and take a few pictures. I still have some of these pictures. After a short time, we were ready to descend. The snow was soft. Our companions, the guests we had met at the hut the day before, were afraid they would slip and therefore came down very slowly. But Paul and I glissaded down in 25 minutes to the hut on the Aldersruhe, and continued to the Oberwalder Hut, where our food was stored.

"The next morning we said our good-byes to our companions. We then left the hut to make our way to the Rudolf Hut through the Odwinkler notch between Johannisberg and Eiskoegele. The trip took five-and-a-half hours. The

(left to right) Paul and Joe with friends on the summit of the Grossglockner.

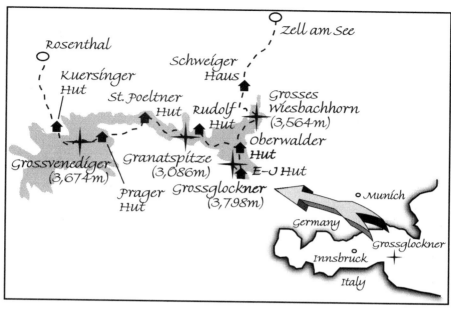

A map showing the brothers' tour through the Austrian Alps in 1922.

Rudolf Hut was very comfortable and at a low elevation, only 2,242 meters.

"Our perfect weather turned stormy. Nonetheless, we aimed for our next goal — the St. Poeltner Hut at 2,555 meters on the Felbertauern. We took a very good trail that passed over the Weis See, Granatspitze, Amertalerhoehe (which is 2,839 meters) and over several other mountain tops between 2,500 and 2,900 meters high. On the last mile along the ridge, called Weinbuechel, the wind was so strong that, at times, we had to lie down so that we would not be blown off the mountain. Then it got foggy. We were very glad when, all at once, after 13 1/2 hours, the St. Poeltner Hut appeared before us, right out of the clouds.

"The hut had a great number of guests who had been driven there from all over the area by the bad weather. We were very hungry and thirsty, but there was no water, and nothing else to drink. The drinking water came from a nearby creek, 200 feet away and about 50 feet below us. The storm was so bad that nobody would go out for water. Finally, Paul and I, the youngest ones in the hut, took the buckets and got some good, ice cold water. We didn't mind being out in the storm for another ten to twelve minutes.

"The next segment of our tour was from the St. Poeltner Hut to the Prager Hut. The trail is called the Poeltnerhoehenweg and goes over the Kesselkopf notch at an elevation of 2,880 meters. It was easy, and it took us only seven hours.

"The following morning, however, the barometer indicated that a new storm was coming. This was unfortunate because we had hoped to get to the top of the Grossvenediger, which is 3,674 meters, and reach the Kuersinger Hut on the other side. We decided to take our chances. The glacier was close to the hut, so we put on our crampons. While we were doing this, a young man, a little older than me, asked us where we were going and if he could join us. We agreed to have him come along.

"No more than a half-an-hour into our journey, it started to snow. Our new companion decided to give up and returned to the hut while it was still within sight. Although visibility was poor, we continued on. It got so bad that we had to use our compass to continue up the mountain. Our ice axes started to sing from the electrical discharge, and there was some lightning. We were in a regular whiteout.

"Just as we thought we were close to the top of Grossvenediger, three men appeared before us out of the fog. They had just made it to the top, but were afraid to climb down to the Kuersinger Hut because of a large cornice they knew to be there, but couldn't see because of the whiteout. They were trying to decide what to do. From our direction and their position, we figured that the descent notch was to our right. Just as we started toward the notch, the sun broke through the clouds for a second, and we could clearly see our way down.

"We led the way and the three men followed us. Soon we were in the front of a big *Randkluft* — a moat — that was blocking our way. By this time, we were below the clouds. We could clearly see a large crevasse, about ten to twelve feet wide, and a lower edge several feet below. There was no snow bridge anywhere around. The snow was soft, and, for a few minutes, we stood on the edge of the crevasse. One of the men asked, 'What are we going to do now?'

"We said, 'Jump it.' Paul belayed me and gave me enough rope to do so. I jumped the cravasse fairly easily — at least, that's how I remember it. For a while the men hesitated, but we told them that if they did not make up their minds, we would leave them. So they decided to jump too. We belayed them, which made them very happy, and they thanked us.

"The rest of the descent to the Kuersinger Hut was easy. By four o'clock, we were drinking tea there, and at around six o'clock, we left for Rosenthal, where we took the train home the next morning.

"When we were riding home on the train and thought about our trip, we were amazed at what happened. Here we were, a couple of kids, and all these people wanted to join us."

Jim Peavler, a student of mountaineering history and of the Stettners, after having heard this story, wrote:

> The two boys who came out of the mountains that evening were not the same ones who had gone in only a few days before. They now were experienced glacier travelers and accomplished route finders. They had already demonstrated traits that were to become trade-marks of the Stettner brothers. First, they share an imperturbable patience. It seems that no matter what the conditions offered, or what might go wrong, outwardly, at least, they quietly and calmly set about solving the problem. Part of their confidence on this trip probably resulted from their mental and physical preparation. The hours spent reading about mountaineering technique and studying maps in Munich probably explain much of the confidence and competence these two inexperienced young men displayed on this, their first major mountaineering trip.

> A second trait that make the Stettners among the most revered of America's early mountaineers is their way with people. I have never met anyone who knows them who would not feel comfortable following either one of them anywhere in the mountains. As early as 1922, when Joe was 21 and Paul only barely 16, something about their demeanor caused people to ask them for guidance in the mountains. These strengths will show up like leitmotifs throughout their lives, and are essential ingredients in what Jack Fralick, their most outstanding chronicler, called "the Stettner Way."

When Joe and Paul returned home from their bold and confidence-expanding adventure, they found Munich to be exactly as they had left it — full of problems and with no real opportunity or security for the "sons of a revolutionary man."

chapter 5

Last climbs in Europe

In September of 1919, Corporal Adolph Hitler was sent by his army superiors to observe a meeting of Anton Drexler's German Workers Party, a small political group in Munich. This party was created and supported by the Thule Society, a secret organization of disgruntled members of the right-wing nobility and the middle classes, whose mission it was to further German nationalism, anti-semitism and to prevent Bolshevism. The party's immediate goal was to gain support among the German working classes. It's symbol was the *Hackenkreuz* or swastika.

Hitler joined this group and soon became its propaganda officer, chief organizer and star orator in the beer halls of Munich. Soon the German Workers Party changed its name to the National Socialist German Workers Party, later known as the Nazi Party. Its members developed a public ideology of nationalism, anti-foreignism and anti-semitism.

In the spring of 1920 Hitler left the army and entirely devoted himself to building and strengthening his party. By 1921, the Nazi Party had grown to 4,500 members and attracted influential Free Corps officers and soldiers, who continued to swell the party's membership. These additions enabled Hitler to found the Storm Troops *(Sturmabteilung)*, a paramilitary formation of former Free Corps members, whose mission it was to protect party gatherings and to physically confront opponents in and out of party assemblies — particularly the Jews and Leftists.

The Nazi Party got a boost from the great German inflation of

1923 that resulted in virtual economic collapse, particularly for the working classes. During this time, the Nazi Party's membership, support, influence and power increased significantly throughout Bavaria.

These were not good times for the sons of a revolutionary man. Although Joe and Paul continued to work at their trades, and were increasingly active in their unions, their thoughts were occupied and their hearts captured by the mountains. Besides, the Alps provided these boys not only with a way of life far removed from the troubles of Munich but also with an escape, perhaps ironically, to a safer world.

Joe and Paul had failed to get to the top of Grossvenediger the previous September. The spring of 1923 brought with it a plan to return to and conquer Grossvenediger. Joe remembers this climb well.

"One of our unforgettable trips was over the Easter holidays, starting on March 30, 1923. This time we had four days to get away on a skiing and climbing trip in the high mountains of Austria. We selected Grossvenediger again. The trip promised to cost us more than we could actually afford, but with careful planning, we felt it could be done.

"Because this is an area of glaciers, we had to take extra equipment along, including a rope and an avalanche cord. The food list was rather simple — some rye bread, sardines, hard sausage, dried fruits and sugar. We could not afford to eat in restaurants or in the huts where we planned to stay. It was only tea or soup that we could afford to buy on a trip such as this.

"The train left at six-o'clock in the morning and went over Kitzbuehl, Neukirchen and then 15 miles further to Rosentahl — the end of the line at that time, and the place where we hoped to start our ski tour to the Kuersinger Hut. We studied the path of the train and the general area and came up with a plan to save enough money to make the trip possible. From Kitzbuehl the train made a long trip around the mountains to Neukirchen — a distance of about 65 miles — while a road travelled from Kitzbuehl over the Jochberg Pass to Neukirchen, which was only 20 to 22 miles long. If we could hike those miles quickly, we could get off the train at Kitzbuel, hike over the Pass and catch the train at Neukirchen, which would then take us to our starting point at Rosentahl. It was a good plan. We could save the train fare from Kitzbuel to Neukirchen and this would make our trip affordable.

"So we tried it this way. We got off the train at Kitzbuehl. There was no snow on the ground and the weather was nice and cold. Unfortunately, our heavy skis slowed us down a little. We walked as fast as we could but arrived in Neukirchen just in time to see the last train to our destination pull out of the railway station.

"Tired as we were, we decided to keep on walking as far as

possible so that we would not fall behind our tight schedule. It got very late and very cold. We entered into the back of a farmer's yard. Leaving our skis outside his hay barn, we climbed in. We had nothing to cover ourselves. All we had was our clothes and an extra sweater, so we burrowed a deep hole in the hay and were almost standing as we slept. We were still cold the next morning when we climbed out of the hay. There to greet us, was the farmer. Feeling guilty about our trespass, I said, 'This is a nice place. Who owns it?'

"'I do. It's mine.' We weren't surprised by his answer.

"But the farmer took pity on us and scolded us for not trying to get in the house. Paul and I never paid the farmer for the use of his barn, but each time we traveled through this area to climb we would stay with him. To compensate him, we fixed things and cleaned and tidied up. Later, the farmer told us that his place kept looking better everytime we stayed there.

"It was nearly seven-o'clock in the morning when we packed up again and continued on our hike to Rosentahl. Our legs were stiff from the day before, but slowly we got into the swing of things.

"From Rosentahl, we started up the trail to our goal — the Kuersinger Hut. At the beginning of our climb, there was no snow on the ground, and we had to carry our skis. Later, however, we reached snow and it felt good to start skiing and use a different set of muscles. After about six hours of skiing, we reached the hut. Now came our surprise — we were not alone. On the contrary, the hut was so full of people that we had to sleep in the unheated attic. Because there were not enough blankets, we had to use parchment paper sheets that we had brought with us. We were cold for a second night.

"The next day we left the hut by 7:30 a.m. for the summit of the Grossvenediger. We soon had to rope up because the crevasses were slightly covered with snow and the snow conditions were not good. After two-and-a-half hours of climbing in bad weather and bad snow conditions, we realized that we could not make the top of Grossvenediger and still get back to Rosentahl to catch the train. We decided to turn back. After skiing back to the hut, we picked up our belongings and, with new snowfall on the ground, we skied nearly all the way back to the railway station at Rosentahl. It took us only four-and-a-half hours.

"We slept that night in the little railroad station on a wooden bench. At six in the morning, we took the train to Neukirchen. Although we hated to get off the train with all our belongings and start walking again, we did so. Once again we took the 22 mile hike over the Jochberg Pass to Kitzbuehl. At Kitzbuehl, we boarded the train and arrived home in Munich late that evening. We were extremely tired. I remember this trip so well. It was the last one that Paul and I took together in Europe.

"Over the years I have often been amused by our last European climb. We really didn't have enough time or money to take the trip. But we were determined. We must have hiked over 90 miles and slept only a few hours during our short trip. And then we froze. Still, we didn't make it to the top of Grossvenediger. So it is with climbing . . . and with life.

"During trips like this our skis always got beaten up. The skis were made of ash, and we had to smooth the wood down with a plane and fix up the edges. Steel edges did not exist then. Paul and I, however, made a device — a very simple metal piece — that we clamped on the edges of our skis. These metal pieces could be used on unbreakable crust. I can make a sketch for you. I think it will make it clear how it was used.

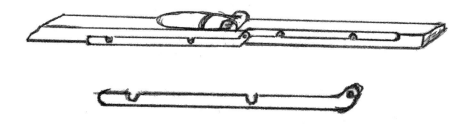

"You see, when this metal piece was not being used, it stayed attached on the side of the ski."[6]

The political and economic problems facing the Stettner family were virtually insurmountable. Work was hard to find, and a working man's wages during the great inflation were horribly inadequate. William Shirer describes the situation:[4]

> The strangulation of Germany's economy hastened the final plunge of the mark. On the occupation of the Ruhr in January 1923, it fell to 18,000 to the dollar; by July 1 it had dropped to 160,000; by August 1 to a million. By November, when Hitler thought his hour had struck, it took four billion marks to buy a dollar, and thereafter the figures became trillions. German currency had become utterly worthless. Purchasing power of salaries and wages was reduced to zero. The life savings of the middle classes and the working classes were wiped out. But something even more important was destroyed: the faith of the people in the economic practices of such a society.

Joe remembers this time. "There was really nowhere in Munich to get away from the nation's economic and political troubles. Even the German-Austrian Alpine Club was political. My group, the Section Neuland, which means the 'New Land Section,' had split from the main club in Munich, because politics was affecting everthing the club was doing. The Section Neuland was opposed to this. Politics was everywhere, even in climbing clubs.

"Our section believed there was no place for politics in the mountains — leave politics and religion behind when you go climbing! But we weren't completely successful at this. Some Nazis became members. That was the way Hitler worked — infiltrate all organizations and groups. It didn't make any difference whether the organizations were labor unions or sport clubs. The Nazis wanted control of them.

"Our family was in trouble, too. One day, my mother ran into her grandson Ernst on the street. This child was my older sister Ernstine's son. The boy greeted her with, 'Heil Hitler!' My mother immediately replied, 'Don't say that to me. Your grandfather was killed by these Nazis.' The boy answered, 'I can report you at school.' His mother was very religious and, like many religious people in Munich at the time, she supported the Right-wing and opposed communism because she thought it was godless. Later Ernst became a prominent Nazi officer with the S.S. He had 'S.S.' tattooed on his arm. After the Second World War, he emigrated to Lebanon. Once, in a letter to me he complained about my using the term 'Israel.' 'Don't mention that word,' he wrote. 'That place doesn't exist.' He apparently hadn't changed.

"The economic problems also were bad for everyone, it seemed. My father had a friend, a Professor Oscheski, who was also a member of the Independent Socialist Party. After my father's death, Professor Oscheski was put in jail. This caused terrible hardships for his family. To ease the financial burden on his family, his son Willi, who was my age and a friend of mine, came to live with us for a while. Several times I gave him money to help him and his family, even though we were experiencing hard times too. After I left Germany, I learned from my mother that the Nazis had arrested Willi and taken him to the prison at Schoddelheim, where they had him beheaded.

"Our family had serious economic problems. For that reason — and because she knew Germany was dangerous for us — my mother decided that it would be better for Paul to emigrate. It was a big family decision. My father had been very active in the union to which Paul, who was at this time also a photoengraver, belonged. A number of influential union members, who were friends of my father, went out of their way to find a job for Paul in Sweden where it would be much safer for him.

Many of these union members had concluded that communism would never work. They believed that, even in the union, everyone only looked out for himself. They had given up on the idea of a communist revolution, and they were happy to help Paul leave. So in 1924, Paul went to Sweden.

"After Paul's departure, I made a few climbs in the Stubaier Alps of Austria, and I took a few ski trips. It wasn't the same without him. I'll tell you about one of those trips.

"It was in the spring of 1925. My records, which were written in pencil and are hard to read, indicate that the trip was taken sometime between the 9th and 14th of April.

"Seven of us from the Section Neuland of the German-Austrian Alpine Club went on the climb. We decided to go to the Stubaier mountains and spend some time around the Dresdner Hut. This is the same hut that Paul and I hiked to, and found closed during Christmas of 1921.

"We arrived in Innsbruck late in the evening and decided to stay there for the night. The next day we took a local train to Fulpmes and arrived by 9:15 in the morning. We were very heavily laden with ropes, food, crampons and ice axes, in addition to our skis. Out of the seven, Ernst Wendl, Hans Urban and I formed a small group and stuck, more or less, together.

As it was spring, much of the snow had already melted, although the upper part of the trail still had some snow. To deal with the lower part, we constructed a little cart that could be assembled and taken apart easily. We still didn't get to the hut until ten-o'clock that night. The hut was open! I felt great relief when I entered. The hut, which was actually a sturdy

Ernst Wendl, Joe (center), and Hans Urban with their gear on a cart at the Fulpmes train station in April of 1925.

The Hildesheimer Hut.

stone house, provided food and a place to sleep. After a good night's rest, we were ready for our skiing trip the next day.

"We decided to travel in the direction of the Hildesheimer Hut, by way of the Schaufelnieder Pass. Hans and I were roped together as we crossed the glacier, and we were not used to this kind of skiing. And we had problems. We had spills. But we made it, though in an exhausted state. After some refreshments and rest, Ernst suggested that, since the weather was good and we were rested, we should try to climb a mountain. We took him up on this, and in an hour or so we were on the top of Schussgrabenvogel (3,310 meters). Once there, Ernst said, 'How about trying the next peak. It's not far away.' We again agreed with him, and so we made the Schaufelspitze (3,333 meters). It was quite worthwhile, but by that time we all felt we had had enough for the day and satisfied, skied down to the Hildersheimer Hut.

"The following day, the entire group decided to climb the Stubaierwildspitze. We knew this climb would involve snow, ice and rock climbing, mostly along a ridge and cornice. The weather was not promising, but we went along anyway. We left our skis at the first steep place and changed to crampons, ice axes and ropes. Shortly, most of the party gave up on their attempts to climb because they thought it too dangerous. Ernst and I, however, roped together and continued on. It was a very exciting climb — we went over ice-covered rocks and snow cornices. In four hours we were standing on top of Stubaierwildspitze.

"We knew what we could expect on the way down, as the snow began to fall and a strong wind blew over the ridge. We had a few apricots to eat, and then shook hands for good luck and started down. Because we felt we had to belay each other, it was slow going. We could hardly see. At one moment my ice ax slipped out of my hand and disappeared over the ridge.

"It became stuck in a rather bad place some 50 to 60 feet below. I did not feel it was worthwhile to go after it, but my friend insisted that we recover it. I belayed him. Although it took him some time, he got the ice ax. Finally, we got off the ridge and located our skis. By this time, it was snowing heavily. It is a wonder that we found the hut. It was a hard day for all of us. Ernst was a real good climbing partner for me. He was strong and we trusted one another.

Joe (at left) and Hans Urban on Joe's last climbing trip in Europe, May of 1925.

"Ernst and I climbed a couple more peaks during the next couple of days and skied back to the Dresdner Hut. It was a nice trip, but I missed Paul.

"A month later Hans Urban and I took a trip to the Allgaeuer Mountains. It was a short trip; but in two days, we hiked in, climbed the Nebelhorn, Wengenkopf and the Grossen and Kleinen Daumen, hiked out and returned to Munich. This, it turned out, was my last climbing trip in Europe.

"By the way, of the three of us, I am the only survivor. Hans died around 1980. At the time, he was the coach for the German Women's Olympic Ski Team. I was able to get in contact with Ernst, and we looked forward to seeing one another. But he died in 1984, before I was able to get to Germany again.

"My mother and our family decided that I, like Paul, should also leave Germany. My mother had a sister, Marie Weber, who lived on the South Side of Chicago. Another aunt loaned me $200. So I traveled to America. When I informed the police of my intention to leave, they asked, 'Why do you want to go to America?'

"I told them that I wanted to have a better life than I could have in Germany. The police told me that I had skills and should stay and help build a stronger Germany. I wasn't moved by their talk. Besides, I had made up my mind and wanted to go."

Joe's answer to the police was not totally candid or complete. Later he explained this move in a letter:

> My reasons were simple — to improve my standard of living, and to get away from the threat of fascism which was getting well on the way with Hitler, Goering, Goebles, and the rest. I knew that in time they would stop at nothing — that they would kill anyone who was against them. I lost my father through the hands of the advance movement of Hitlerism. I am sure that I would have had a hard time surviving if I had remained in Munich.

Joe and Paul left Munich and a world fraught with brutal political upheaval. Soon, Paul would join Joe in Chicago. Then, both in America, they would be free to work in relative peace and turn their sights to a new set of mountains, well designed to rekindle their intense passion for climbing.

chapter 6

America at Last

Joe was not particularly happy during his first year in America. Pursuant to plan, he moved in with his aunt, who lived in a small frame house on the South Side of Chicago. Typical of Germans living in America after the Great War, Joe's aunt and her family spoke only English. As Joe put it, "They didn't want to speak German to anyone. My aunt spoke both German and English, but she rarely spoke any language at all. My cousins were born here and spoke English." Having never learned English, Joe felt out of place. He felt he had no real family, no workable language, no Paul and no mountains.

He set about solving the problems. "I decided I didn't want to speak German anymore, so I started to speak only English. I found work doing odds and ends, including carpentry, plumbing and heating. I fixed the pipes in my neighbor's house. Hardly anyone knew how to do the metal work. When others learned that I could do this, it helped me find more jobs. I did what ever I could to make money. I sent a quarter of my income back home for my mother and family there. She was suffering financially because of my father's death and the German inflation.

"My aunt found a place for me in the attic, which was swelteringly hot in the summer. I cut a hole in the attic to permit minimal airflow. I paid my aunt rent for this accommodation.

"I missed Paul more and more. So I 'worked on him' to convince him to leave Stockholm and come to America. During this time, I learned about a metal worker's union and joined it. This affiliation

*Paul (at left) and Joe,
together again in
Chicago, 1926.*

resulted in regular employment until my retirement.

"My aunt's dominating concern was religion — hers and mine. She was very, very religious. It was her only passion in life. She took advantage of nearly every service and religious opportunity her church offered and was disappointed, even angry, that I did not. I shared neither her fervor nor her belief. Nonetheless, I attended church, mainly to assure peace in the household.

"Eventually it got to be too much. So I took to skipping church. My aunt grew suspicious. She asked if I had attended church. I resorted to lying as a means of keeping matters smooth. She was not convinced by my lies. She became intent on exposing my fraud and started interrogating me about what had occurred at church and about my opinion of events and homilies. Her interrogation was successful; my sin was exposed and matters only got worse.

"I was more successful with Paul. He succumbed to my urgings and came to my rescue. He arrived in Chicago in late 1926. There wasn't enough room in the attic for both Paul and I. So we explained to our aunt that it was necessary to find accommodations elsewhere. I didn't say 'and liberty,' but that's what I thought.

"Soon we found a rooming house on the North Side of Chicago, some 100 blocks away from my aunt's house. We could wash and cook in our new room. It was near Lincoln Avenue and Halsted. It was a mixed neighborhood with a large population of Germans.

"The year I spent with my aunt had been hard. I settled with her financially, and Paul and I threw ourselves into our new life. I didn't see my aunt again until just before the Second World War, when my mother came to visit.

"Almost the moment that Paul set foot in Chicago, he began to worry about transportation. 'How are we going to get around?,' he wanted to know. Paul had had a little motorcycle in Sweden, and he thought we ought to get motorcycles. I was skeptical.

"After a while he convinced me. At least he convinced me to take a look. We went to a dealer, where Paul found a used Indian that looked good. Paul said, 'That's a good motorcycle, but we need two.' The dealer just happened to have another Indian in the back. Paul liked them and, without even talking with me about it, said, 'We'll take both of them.'

"I was stunned. Now I had a motorcycle. I whispered to Paul, 'I don't know how to ride a motorcycle!'

"'That's OK,' he replied. 'I'll drive one home and come back and get the other.' These two motorcycles cost us $400 each. I still have the receipt. It was cheap transportation. Gas was only 17 cents a gallon. Our trip to Colorado and back in 1927 probably didn't cost us more than eight dollars.

"I took a number of falls learning how to ride the motorcycle. But I learned. Paul and I went all over Chicago, probably frightening everyone. Then we started to take longer trips. Eventually we rode to the Mississippi River and then to Wisconsin.

"Soon after settling in our new neighborhood, we met Germans from all over Germany. We joined the *Naturfreunde* (Friends of Nature), a predominately German-American hiking and social club in communities with large German populations.

"The Naturfreunde decided to build a house on the Indiana Sand Dunes, like the huts in the Alps. Nearly every weekend, Paul and I went there to help build it.

"No one in the club did any climbing. But when Paul arrived, he and I took off on our motorcycles and soon discovered Devils Lake in Wisconsin. There are no mountains there, but it seemed like a good place to practice rock climbing. We were likely the first to rock climb there. Now it's very popular and very crowded. Soon, we invited friends from Naturfreunde to go climbing with us at Devils Lake. Scrambling on the cliffs around the lake soon became an important part of Naturfreunde outings.

"At first, Paul couldn't find a job as a photoengraver. This made him angry. I told him not to worry about this because I was making enough to support us both for a while. This was not acceptable for Paul.

He continued to complain. I showed him how to do some metal work, which got him some work. But he wanted to be a photoengraver.

"Paul was aggressive and after a while he got an 'open' job as an engraver for about six months. At that time, the photoengraver's union went on strike. Paul supported the union and their strike. This helped them accept him, and he became a member of the union. We were now both making money, which made longer trips possible.

"We wanted to travel to and climb a mountain that had 'respect'. We knew that Colorado had such mountains. We had no particular desire to climb Longs Peak, but we had heard about it and knew that it had challenging climbs. So we decided to go there and see it. Paul and I also wanted to do something different, climb something that hadn't been done before.

"We didn't have any climbing equipment. So we ordered some from Germany. We didn't order a rope, because, we thought, there are mountains and mountain climbers in Colorado, and we can get a rope there. And, of course, we didn't want to load up our motorcycles even more.

"So we made our plans. September is a good time for climbing in the Alps, and we thought it would be a good time in Colorado. We saved our money.

"In the middle of the summer, I told my boss about our plans to take a vacation. He said, 'We don't take vacations here.' I told him that we were going anyway, so I got fired. As it turned out, it wasn't so bad. He rehired me when I returned. This pattern was repeated several times over the years when Paul and I wanted to go climbing.

"That's what I remember of my first year in America."

chapter 7

The Stettner Ledges

Joe was relaxed as he sat in his chair in his living room. "So you want to hear about our climb up the ledges on the East Face of Longs Peak," he said. "Most climbers want to hear about that climb. A little while ago, Ginnie found the journal I kept of our 1927 trip to Colorado. It's about the Longs Peak climb. It's in German, but you should be able to deal with it. I think it'll tell you more than I can now remember. I also have a few pages written by Paul."

Joe's daughter Ginnie hunted for the journal and Paul's notes. She found them. What follows is my translation of Joe's journal, supplemented by some of Paul's notes about the "Ledges" and Joe's memories:

"It was Saturday, September 3, 1927, as we equipped our two Indian motorcycles for the trip. Several months before, we had ordered climbing equipment (mostly pitons) from Germany. These items arrived only a few hours before our planned departure, already a sign of good fortune. Several friends were taking a trip to the Sand Dunes on Lake Michigan, and, at the very last moment, we wanted to see them once again at the railroad station.

"We jumped on our wheels and tried, as quickly as possible, to get to the train station. In the heat of this action, a taxi suddenly stopped right in front of me. Other than a scratch on my gas tank and a minor injury to my hand, nothing serious happened. Although this did not delay us, it wasn't possible to get to the railroad station in time.

Joe (at left) and Paul fuel up in Chicago on their departure for the Rockies in 1927.

"It was already afternoon when we left the city. Our first goal was "Starved Rock," which is about 105 miles away. We rode away without additional delay and reached our camping site at about nine o'clock in the evening. We set up our tent. After satisfying our stomachs, we crept into the feathers of our sleeping bags.

"The day broke with a lingering fog everywhere. Like ghosts, tourists sprang up everywhere. They all had foolishly frozen in their tents, as we had. While we ate our breakfast, we took down the tent and again packed everything securely on our motorcycles' luggage racks.

"'Today we should cover a good distance.' Merrily we began the trip. A good concrete road went through LaSalle and then to Davenport, the first large city we passed through. We had left the State of Illinois. Iowa's roads consist of loam and, as a consequence, are not well-suited for motorcycles, as I shall later show.

"On Illinois' roads we drove at a speed of 70 miles per hour, whereas here 25 to 30 miles was a good performance. Holes, bumps and ditches predominated along these Iowa roads. Paul crashed and cut his knee. So, during the entire trip, he carried a souvenir of Iowa.

"Our next campsite was supposed to be farther west, but on this day, we decided we had gone far enough. Besides, the little town offered us a beautiful place to camp.

"The next morning brought with it beautiful weather. After completing the daily work of washing, cooking and packing, etc., we departed this small, but very pretty town. We resolved not to decide how far we wanted to go that day because we had no idea what the roads would be like. We had 600 miles on our odometer when Paul, just before Omaha, Nebraska, encountered a nail with his rear tire. Also, my oil pump was not working properly, so we took a short break for repairs. Then we went on and found ourselves in Nebraska.

"The roads were better in Nebraska, though still not very good. By afternoon the sky darkened, and it began to storm. We tried to get out of the storm zone by driving fast, but our speed didn't help us. The cloud burst so great that it almost washed us away into the ditch. We held our ground, but our suits, designed to be waterproof, proved to be just the opposite. As a fitting end to this scene, our motorcycles also got flooded. And we found ourselves standing in streaming sunshine in open fields.

"We were once again successful in bringing our motorcycles back to life. We were able to fix one cylinder of the two, which got us to the next camp site about a mile from Ames.

"The night was noteworthy, with continuous lightning that caused us to suspect the worst. As soon as the rain let up a little, we pitched our tent under a tree.

"Several minutes from our tent, we had seen a small cafe. We wanted something warm to drink before we went to sleep, so we headed for the cafe where we sat for a couple of hours. Outside the wind and rain raged so fiercely that we decided to stay. Two tramps joined us. They said they had found a place to stay that night with a farmer and asked us where we were sleeping. We assured them that we had a beautiful and dry place in our tent and did not wish to trade sleeping places with them. It could rain and storm as much as it liked. We were protected.

"Our assurances were most boastful, as we would soon see. We left the cafe rather late and searched for our tent. Then the shock. The tent had disappeared and all of our clothing, blankets, etc., were rooted all around. Water stood nearly two inches deep in our tent. There was no dry spot to be found. With time, it became clear to us that hungry dogs had spoiled our food and brought total chaos to our tent. Since there was no hotel in the area, the only remaining alternative for us was to sleep in our wet things.

"We were in luck because the next morning, the sun was once again shining with laughter upon us. We quickly prepared to go and turn our backs to this place, when something else occurred. My magneto somehow failed and the motor simply would not start. After three hours, Paul succeeded in overcoming the mischief. The point on the magneto was rusted, because on the previous day, water had penetrated the motor from all sides.

"The next 16 miles were not pleasant. There were deep mud holes all over the road. After a while, matters got better. We encountered sand roads, which were firmer. We passed through a number of small towns, including Grand Island and Kearney. We also crossed the Platte River several times, as we had been following this waterway since Omaha.

"We reached the town of Overton, and the campsite there allowed us a good night's rest. The next day was, in general, not bad. There may have been some variation, but I can't remember it well enough to describe. Nebraska had become so boring.

"Shortly after Big Springs, we left Nebraska and rode into Colorado. By the end of the day, we were able to go as far as Crook, Colorado, where we hurriedly put up our tent and then took a short walk past the few houses in the town.

"The next morning was as we wished. Nature had awakened, and the day that stood before us promised new experiences and beauty. But the next 142 miles were over bad roads. Often we had to drive over sand that had drifted to a height of six to nine inches. Paul and I alternated crashes with considerable industry. Neither our motorcycles nor we suffered serious damage from these numerous falls.

The brothers first spot the Rockies on their 1927 trip to Colorado.

"By mid-afternoon, we passed through Denver. It was a great feeling to see some mountains again after two years. It had been even longer since Paul and I had climbed together in Austria. Without even stopping, we left Denver so that we could reach Colorado Springs that same day. We had to cover 80 more miles that afternoon.

"An automobile passed us on the outside, challenging us indirectly to test our motorcycles after this long trip. We were 15 miles from Colorado Springs before the road became good again, and the auto had nearly disappeared from our eyes. So we resolved to catch this 'wheel barrow.' 1 - 2 - 3 and 60 miles per hour, faster it called us, and we turned on the gas until the pointer on the speedometer was pushed to over 80 miles-an-hour. But at about five miles before Colorado Springs, we reached our destination for the day, which required us to turn off and let the 'wheel barrow' go past as we reduced our tempo.

"In good spirits, we pulled into Camp Rodeo and rented a little cabin that offered fine accommodations for several days. We had a good meal and today, once again after a long period, we had a bed. We planned to get up very early. Pikes Peak at 14,109 feet above sea level was on our minds, and we wanted to climb it on our motorcycles.

"As I explained, we had planned to get up early. We were therefore very surprised to see the sun shining through the window of our hut. We quickly wished our campsite good day and started to pack our motorcycles for the mountain trip. Traveling very fast, we rode through Colorado Springs until the last houses disappeared behind us. Immediately our motorcycles had their first test to pass. The road was rather steep with numerous curves until we reached the settlement of Cascade. In the course of our fast ride, we overlooked the entrance to Pikes Peak and drove to the next mountain town, Green Mountain Falls. We took several photographs, and then thoughtlessly drove down the wrong road until we discovered that we had traveled ten miles too far.

"Soon we discovered the right way, and we were on our way to Pikes Peak and the highest automobile road in the world. Our motorcycles withstood the incline easily, and we continued our trip to the inn at Glen Cove at 11,425 feet above sea level. After a short rest, we continued on our journey. Our steel horses functioned as ever. In spite of the great, rather time-consuming climb we had to overcome, we reached the summit at 14,109 feet. We had subdued Pikes Peak with our motorcycles.

"A glorious view was the reward for our effort. The very cold temperature on the summit admonished us to quickly turn around. The return trip was without incident, although suddenly the weather worsened. Just as we arrived at the foot of the mountain, we noticed that the summit

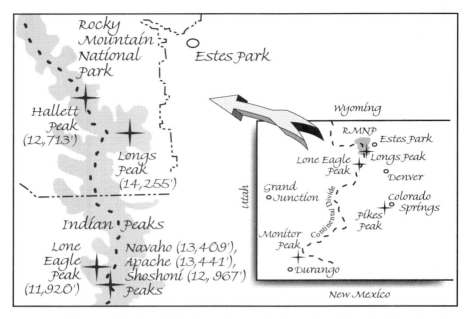

A map of Joe and Paul's 1927 trip to Longs Peak in the Colorado Rockies, also showing the locations of Lone Eagle Peak (1933) and Monitor Peak (1947).

of Pikes Peak was covered with a magnificent white.

"We returned quite early to our cabin at Camp Rodeo. After inspecting our motorcycles, we had our evening meal and sent about 30 or 40 postcards in all directions. Then we jumped into our folding beds.

"Again we slept late. When we awoke, we gathered equipment for a new trip to the Garden of the Gods (a sandstone maze that was transformed into fantastic figures during the Ice Age.) We wanted to do some warm-up climbs before heading for Longs Peak's East Face. Different jagged peaks in the Garden of the Gods invited us to an airy climbing fest. We nearly spent the entire day climbing, photographing and patching up our pants (torn by the sharp rocks.)

"Before we left this area, we met several Indians who managed to make a living by selling hand-made rugs, vases, shoes, and sewn articles. These Indians had been deprived of their land by self-proclaimed civilized peoples.

"We had neither the time nor means to visit such places as the Cave of the Winds, the Cliff Dwellings, Buffalo Bill's Grave, etc. But, as nature lovers, we declined to purchase admission to these attractions in preference to the beauty of Nature, and the opportunity to visually appreciate it. The sinking sun caused us to again find our place of lodging.

"The next day was a day of rest for us. Our trip back to Denver, and farther to Golden, was relaxed and pleasant. The following day we reached Longmont, where we set up another camp. The next day would bring our goal, Longs Peak, close to us.

"The morning was wonderful as we continued our journey to the Longs Peak Inn. In each town we passed, we searched in vain for a climbing rope to purchase, which we needed to complete our climbing equipment. This surprised us – in Germany and Austria you can always get a rope in the mountain villages. But not here in America. Our last hope was in the Alpine Information Bureau at the Longs Peak Inn.

There was a rope at the Inn, but the owner refused to sell it or let us use it. He thought it was too late in the season to undertake such a dangerous climb. We tried to prove to them that we were experienced climbers and that we had everything but a rope. But we couldn't budge them. Thus, here too our wishes and efforts were for naught. Without a rope, our plan was most certainly not feasible.

"Not only did we not get the rope, we were advised against attempting any climb on the East Face of Longs Peak. They told us that there had been several serious falls on this wall and, of the eight parties that attempted to climb it this year, only one had been successful. And that climb was on Alexander's route.[5]

"Because we could not get a rope, and because our food was nearly gone, we decided to drive to Estes Park. This time we were successful. In the corner of the general store, we found some sisal hemp rope – a big coil, 1/2-inch thick, stiff and heavy. We bought 120 feet of it. Though not the best, it ought to fulfill the purpose.

"With a sense of victory and inner satisfaction, we reached, on the same day, a campsite just above Charley Hewes' Kirkwood Inn at 8,000 feet. Just as we were about to set up our tent, a park ranger surprised us. He had heard that we planned to climb a route on the East Face and suggested that we go higher to the Timberline Cabin (at Jim's Grove) at 11,050 feet, where we would have decent quarters. We covered our *iron horses* with the tent and put our packs on our back.

"We had a three-and-half-mile steep hike ahead of us and the weather appeared to worsen. What troubled us the most was the fact that, as we hurried to the protection of the cabin, the sky became increasingly dark. We knew that a powerful storm was coming. And then, we looked up and, by sheer luck, we saw the hut a hundred yards in the distance. We soon found ourselves under its roof.

"The cabin was in a powerful state of disorder. It was much worse than the huts in the Alps, but better than our pup tent. First we covered the broken windows with some paper. Then we improved the

Joe (at left) and Paul at the Timberline Cabin. Note their climbing gear hung on the wall behind the stove.

roof to hinder the cold and rain from entering. Paul was successful in setting up a small stove, and prepared a hot drink. In a short time, this fortress was brought into order. The only thing we mountain rats lacked was good music. After packing our backpacks for the next day, we stretched out on the sacks of straw to sleep.

"September 14, 1927: The storm raged the entire night. The wind howled and shook the cabin. It was so powerful that we often thought the cabin would be blown off its foundation. At 5:00 a.m., we once again had clear skies — the wind having driven away all the clouds. It was a promising day for our climb.

"After about an hour or so, we reached Chasm Lake, which lies at about 12,000 feet. Then we skirted over boulders around the north end of the lake and went farther to a small glacier (Mills Glacier) beneath the East Face. At this point, we stopped to choose our route. We were familiar with two established climbing routes on the East Wall — Kieners and Alexanders. We studied them. But we wanted to find a new route. We searched for a route by looking at Alexanders Chimney and working our way to the right with the binoculars. With the help of these field glasses, we found a line of broken plates, ledges and cracks that we could eventually use as a route. It looked challenging enough for us. Many places on the route didn't appear to have any climbing potential. We knew, however, that when we were closer, it would look more favorable. We finally decided to ascend via these ledges as close as possible to the left of the water markings coming down from Broadway — the big ledge, 1,000 feet higher, that runs across the entire East Face.

"It didn't appear to us to be all that difficult, although I had some concerns about the places that were iced up. When I expressed this concern to Paul, he responded, 'We can worry about that when we get there.'

"It was getting late, and we didn't know how much time we needed. There was not much time to waste. So, equipped with ice axes, crampons and the necessary rock climbing tools, we worked our way up the steep fields of hard, frozen snow that led to a good place to begin our climb. On the way, we had to cut several steps. At that point, in place of our *nailed-affairs* (hobnailed boots), we next donned our felt-soled rock climbing shoes. We did not wish to leave all our snow and ice equipment there, because eventually we would make a long descent down the North Face. Besides, crampons and a camera provide the necessary ballast. I bundled up our ice axes and some of our food, and slid these things down the steep snow field to be picked up later.

"We made a cairn at this place, and then got to work. Paul had, in the interim, taken off unroped and worked his way up 100 feet higher, while I was heavily loaded with a *blutsau getsda graisle* (blood sucking[7]). We overcame the first obstacles.

"At first, I thought this was not the way to climb the route, but Paul climbed this section quite securely. Paul slowed down a bit, and I was soon able to catch up to him. When we were once again together, I said to Paul, 'All right, you lead, but take the rope and put it on, and keep it on the rest of the way.' We then tied into the rope. With great trouble, we fought our way upwards. Time-wise, it appeared that we would have to retreat. The wall was approximately 1,600 feet high and, besides being steep, it had many overhanging sections."

Paul's comments about the climb are added here. "Slowly we made our way over smooth slabs. The view down the steep wall to the snowfield far below was wonderful. All around us was deep silence, broken only by a call from one of us to the other, or the sound of the hammer being used on a piton. Occasionally there was a bombardment of rocks and ice chunks, which called for extra caution. Often it was necessary for me to rid myself of my knapsack in order to scale an overhang or a spot with only a few holds. Joe then had both knapsacks to carry, or we pulled them up on the rope. On one of the overhangs, he had been overloaded and warned me to that effect. I held the rope taut and he swung in midair. After I gave him a few meters of rope, he was

Joe works his way up the wall on Stettner Ledges, September of 1927.

able to rest for another attempt."

Joe also wrote about this moment in his journal, but with greater emotion. "On one overhanging section, I was in trouble. My strength was exhausted and my backpacks pulled me unmercifully into the depths. It made me feel very unbalanced. I yelled up to Paul, 'HOLD TIGHTLY! I'M FALLING !' My cry soon became a reality. I pealed off the rock. Fortunately, Paul had a good belay place and was able to hold me well. The rope around my waist wrung me totally together, like a wet rag, until about 18 feet lower, I was finally able to hold my feet securely on the wall.

"Occasionally we thought it was impossible. At one point, it was necessary to hammer in three pitons to make it possible for Paul, who was leading, to get over this part. There were many, very difficult parts to overcome."

Paul's notes are again added. "We were forced to make frequent use of the pitons, as there was a scarcity of natural securings. Often it was impossible to find cracks for pitons, making it necessary for me to climb greater stretches without much security. I could not afford to let myself slip. Coming to one exceptionally smooth rock, it seemed impossible for us to continue. I hammered in a piton[8], and Joe climbed up to me. Very slowly I worked myself up a few meters more, but my strength gave out. My fingers gave way, and so did my toes, and I found myself going down. Through friction my speed was lessened, and Joe, who was stationed at the piton, brought me to a stop. Several of our pitons are still in that wall, as we could not possibly remove them. Everything had gone well and so, after a short rest, we tried again and succeeded. Soon the upper part of the wall was enshrouded in clouds, and it began to snow. Fortunately, we had the greatest part of the climb behind us. The last section was, in comparison, relatively easy. After five hours of climbing, we stood on Broadway.

"We erected a cairn, took a short rest and then started out again. Keeping to the right, close to the snow filled couloir, over the various pinnacles and chimneys, we finally reached the easy, step-like terrain."

Joe's journal continues, "Were we not so well equipped, we could not have succeeded in reaching the summit, at 4,300 meters (14,255 feet), in six or seven hours. We already had had enough of freezing and, in the last hours of our ascent, it began to snow. Upon reaching the summit at about five-o'clock in the afternoon, we shook hands and recorded our climb in the register. We decided to stop for a short break and ate bread and sardines, our only meal of the day.

"The increasing darkness admonished us to make a quick descent. Although we knew little about the route down the North Face, we knew what direction north was. We made a wild journey over this face. It was not terribly steep, and we nearly ran. There was a lot of snow, but our hobnailed shoes gave us good footing. Just as we thought that we could not go any farther, we discovered, by chance, a steel cable that was anchored in the wall. After descending the cable, we found a footpath. We still had several hours to hike to again reach our hut. Upon our

The East face of Longs Peak. Routes: 1 Stettner Ledges with finish on Alexanders Chimney, 2 Hornsby Direct finish of Stettner Ledges, 3 Alexanders Chimney, 4 Kieners Route, 5 Joe's Solo on Teeter-Totter Pillar, and 6 Joe's Solo as initially presumed (see Chapter 9). (Courtesy the Colorado Mountain Club)

arrival at eight-o'clock in the evening, we quickly fixed a little meal. It had been a good day — a successful day — but we were tired. Soon there was again peace for us in this little house.

"A new day dawned. We went back to retrieve our climbing equipment that we had left behind on the small glacier below the East Face. By late afternoon, we had packed our belongings and were hiking down to our abandoned motorcycles. It was totally dark as we reached this place. We pitched our tents, and again we had to bivouac out in the open.

"At the beginning of the night it was not too cold, but after a short time, we began to shiver in a respectful manner. Our thin blankets were not warm enough. Paul asked me for the candle lantern. I quickly found it hidden under the blankets. He lit it and kept it burning under his blanket to warm himself. This was good enough for Paul, but I was still freezing. Then a silly solution became obvious. I jumped out of the tent, got a can of solid alcohol we used for cooking from my backpack and, using an empty tin can, rigged up a little oven in the tent. After burning my fingers on my oven, I gave up on the idea of patenting my warmth spreader and threw it out of the tent. In the meantime, the warmth had sent Paul quickly to a sound sleep.

"But I could not find any sleep. Before the sun sent its first rays over the summit of Longs, I was on my feet and working hard. The strong flowing mountain stream provided me a refreshing bath. While Paul was still stretched out in the tent, I prepared a breakfast of tea and stale sandwiches. Then we packed our motorcycles and drove first to the Kirkwood Inn where we told the proprietor Charley Hewes, the poet of the Rockies, about our climb and our safe return. Then we rode down the valley into Estes Park, where we were drawn anew to the solitary splendor of Colorado's National Park.

"We landed at Bear Lake and found good lodging in the tourist hotel there. We slept again, this time in white linened beds. Although

Initially only a few people knew about the Stettners' climb, including Charley Hewes (center) shown here with the brothers in 1942.

the day did not promise particularly good weather, we wanted to take a short hike to Hallett Peak and Flat Top. With light packs, we left our lodging and soon reached Nymph Lake, and later Dream Lake at 9,900 feet. Our route led us through weathered forests.

"We were barely above Emerald Lake at 10,200 feet when the desolate talus fields began. We worked our way up several hundred feet higher when suddenly it began to hail and storm. We sought shelter under some rocks, so that we could stay dry enough to continue on our way. The bad weather did not prevent us from climbing to the summit of Hallett, which is 12,700 feet high. There was hardly any view from the top, so we descended again and traversed over to Flat Top, which is at 12,300 feet. We finally succeeded in reaching our starting point at the Bear Lake Lodge. We spent the next several days fishing near the lodge.

"On September 19, 1927, we left this place. 'Live well!,' we said to the mountains of Colorado. We did not know how long it would be before we would see them again. Over numerous curves, we descended down the valley, passed through Estes Park and followed the road through the famous Thompson Canyon. This narrow, hollowed-out canyon stands next to none other.

"By the time night arrived, we found ourselves beyond the view of the mountains. A flat tire forced us to pitch our tent in an open field where only cacti grew. We awoke the next morning fairly frozen and found our motorcycles covered with hoar-frost. We covered 50 miles and reached Sterling, Colorado, where we warmed up and fortified ourselves in a cafe.

"We left this town driving briskly until we had to stop. Paul had let the oil run out of the motor, and it was dry. The motor burned up. No one in Sterling could repair it. I had to pull him, 20 feet behind me, with our climbing rope for 450 miles, until we finally reached Omaha, Nebraska. During this part of the trip home, we took many spills on the gravel roads that, under normal circumstances, would not have taken place. Nearly every time I looked back, Paul was in the ditch. We averaged about 10 to 15 miles an hour. In Omaha, we found the first repair shop, where it took two days to repair the damage.

"On September 24, 1927, at ten-o'clock in the evening, we learned about approaching bad weather. We turned our backs on Omaha and drove the entire night in an effort to beat the rain and storms. We had lost so much time and had to reach Chicago as soon as possible. Soon we hit rain, and found ourselves in Iowa.

"The roads in Iowa are, for the most part, composed of earth and loam. As a consequence, our wheels sunk into dirt. By employing evasions, we managed to go more than a 100 miles through this. Finally, with great fatigue, after three days, we were able to turn our backs on Iowa as well. We found ourselves once again in Illinois.

"It was September 27, 1927, at 5:00 p.m. We were 200 miles from Chicago when the rain caught up with us. Although it rained relentlessly, the concrete roads allowed us to reach Chicago and bring our trip to an end. Thoroughly soaked, we arrived home at two-o'clock in the morning and without any broken bones. We had planned to take a three week vacation. It took us three days longer. The climbing was fun. We overcame a lot of difficulties. We had seen and experienced much. The memories will remain with us forever.

"HAIL TO FREEDOM IN THE MOUNTAINS AND ON THE OPEN ROADS. AMEN!"

Joe's journal shows the determination of the two Stettner boys to try and succeed in climbing a new, and adventurous, route on Longs Peak. They knew what they could accomplish and nothing was going to discourage them. At the same time, it shows how modest they were about their mountaineering achievement.

Joe and Paul hardly mentioned a thing about their climb. They told Charley Hewes, poet and author of *Songs of the Rockies* and later, Joe's dear friend. Hewes told his friend Walter Kiener, a Swiss mountaineer and the pioneer of *Kieners Route* on the East Face, about their climb. Kiener, in turn, looked up Joe and Paul and inquired about it. But other than Hewes and Kiener, no one knew about the climb. As William Bueler in *Roof of the Rockies* wrote, "The Stettners did nothing to publicize the climb, and for several years, its existence was known only to a handful of Longs Peak intimates."

Even the Longs Peak guides were unaware of the Stettners' climb until 1935, when several climbers attempted to repeat the route. One of those climbers took a serious fall, broke his foot and, with some difficulty, was rescued. This contributed to a growing Stettner legend, and to the mystery that began to surround these two climbers. It was not until 1936 that the route was climbed a second time by Warren Gorrell and party. The third ascent was not conducted until 1942, when Joe himself led the climb with Bob Ormes, protégé of Colorado climbing great Albert Ellingwood.

Although Joe and Paul may have felt little need to talk about their climb, others have had plenty to say about the route that was later to become known as the Stettner Ledges.

World-renowned climber Fritz Wiessner set out to perform the climb in 1938, but later, upon inquiry by Jack Fralick just before Wiessner gave a program about his 1939 attempt to climb K-2, he complained that he could not even find the route.

Joe (at left) with Bob Ormes at the third ascent of Stettner Ledges in 1942.

Chris Jones, in his book *Climbing In North America,* called it, ". . . the most demanding climb in the United States up to that time." Author Bernard Gillett, in *Rocky Mountain National Park: The Climber's Guide,* agrees:

> A major accomplishment for its time, Stettners Ledges was the hardest climb in Colorado for twenty years, and perhaps the hardest climb in America of such length when it was put up.

Bob Godfrey and Dudley Chelton, in their book *Climb! Rock Climbing in Colorado* had this to say:

> Stettners Ledges became, and has remained, a classic ascent. In 1927 it was the most difficult Colorado high mountain rock climb and probably the most difficult in the United States . . . Ellingwood's ascent of Lizard Head some seven years prior to the Stettners' climb was comparable in technical difficulty . . . These two climbs were the most advanced technical rock routes in Colorado in the 1920s. No other climbs were to occur in Colorado until the mid-1940s surpassing them in daring and technical difficulty.

Walter Fricke, in his 1971 book *Climbers' Guide to Rocky Mountain National Park,* rated the climb at 5.7. He advises, "a confident climber [to] carry three pitons, eight slings, one nut, and ten carabiners to supplement the many pitons already in place." Then he writes:

> The Stettner Ledges act as a scupper for all the mountain above it, including the large Joe's Solo Couloir, and the effects of rain, hail and snow are thereby magnified. Since most of the route faces north, verglas is to be expected in early and late summer. While the Piton Ladder is often done on aid, one should know that the first ascent was done free. This route was for more than 20 years by far the hardest climb around. Time and modern technique have hardly made it any easier.

Bueler in *Roof of the Rockies* adds:

> For two decades the most difficult route in Colorado was Stettners Ledges on the lower half of the East Face of Longs Peak . . . Yet, since the immigrant Stettners had learned their climbing in the German and Austrian Alps and climbed at the standards prevailing there, their Longs ascent cannot be said to represent Colorado climbing of the time; it was more than a decade ahead of local standards.

Joe once said that the Stettner Ledges was harder than any climb he and Paul had ever done in Europe. It should be remembered that they climbed the route "free," using their small number of pitons only for protection, not as "artificial aid," a climbing method by which climbers use protection for hand and footholds. They also climbed with *manchon*, a kind of felt-sole for rock climbing shoes.[9] Even though a difficulty rating of 5.7 seems quite intermediate by modern standards, one can wonder how today's climbers would fare on the Stettner Ledges with manchon, instead of today's sticky-rubber climbing shoes, with a couple of pitons, instead of numerous, spring-loaded camming devices of all sizes, and with a stiff, one-half inch hemp, 120-foot long cowboy rope, instead of a light, 10mm, 165-foot perlon climbing rope.

Even today, 70 years later, the Ledges inspire awe and enthusiasm, as is clearly suggested by Dougald MacDonald's article on the Stettner Ledges and the Notch Couloir in the June-August 1996 issue of *Climbing*. Although the article contains some historical inaccuracies, such as who led (Paul led every pitch) and a Notch Couloir finish (they finished via Upper Kieners), it reflects modern thinking about the quality and promise of Joe and Paul's route. "It's a classic," MacDonald claims.[9]

In the summer 1996, a luncheon was held at the Aspen Lodge near Estes Park in honor of Joe. It was a perfect setting. The guests could look out of the lodge's large window, across broad meadows and above pine forests to the imposing, awe-inspiring East Face of Longs Peak. It was a given that the conversation would soon turn to the brothers' climb of theLedges 70 years earlier — but first, some background about this conversation.

If one studies the route description of the Stettner Ledges in the several climbers' guide books covering the area, one notes that, toward the top of the Stettner Ledges route, the route traverses off to the left and joins Alexanders Chimney on the way to Broadway. Richard DuMais, in *High Peaks: A Climbing Guide to Mountains of Rocky Mountain National Park,* describes the Stettner Ledges this way, "From the left of the ledge the climb goes up some flakes and then angles up to the left to connect with Route 52 [Alexanders Chimney], which it follows to Broadway." More recently, a direct line was established that goes from the veer-off point straight up to Broadway. This new line, considered a harder variation of the Stettner Ledges, is called the Hornsby Direct. Bernard Gillett, in his book, agrees with DuMais. Discussing the Hornsby Direct variation, Gillett writes that, "the original line [of the Stettner Ledges] diagonalled left to finish on Alexanders Chimney."

During this luncheon conversation, one of the guests asked Joe if he and Paul had considered going straight up, as Hornsby did on his direct route, to Broadway rather than diagonally off to join Alexander's route. Joe casually remarked, "Oh, we did go straight up. Hornsby Direct is part of Stettner Ledges."

Nearly 70 years after Joe and Paul did their climb, we discover that this so-called direct variation of the Stettner Ledges was first climbed by Joe and Paul in 1927, and that their climb was even harder than previously had been known. What was it about the Stettner brothers that explains their reticence to tell others about their climbs?

Some time ago I told Joe that I had done his climb. He said, "I hope you had as much fun as Paul and I did." This simple response tells much about Joe and his attitude toward climbing. As he often has told me, "You should climb for the fun and joy of it. There is no other reason." This also may explain some of brothers' apparent modesty. As the American climbing community would someday learn, the Stettner boys were interested in climbing, not in publicizing. And the "Ledges" was not the only climb the Stettner boys had in mind.

chapter 8   *Marriage and Mountains*

Even the most free-spirited of climbers sooner or later finds his or her style compromised by close encounters of the first kind. So it was with Joe and Paul.

Paul met Anne Frese in 1929 at a get-together of the Naturfreunde. A year later, during the summer of 1930, Paul took Anne to Colorado. On July Fourth, Anne's birthday, they climbed Alexanders Chimney on Longs Peak. It was her first climb, and she didn't know exactly what to expect. But she learned upon reaching the summit. Paul proposed and Anne accepted, a testament to the potency of the mixture of love and hypoxia. So Paul's elaborate plan succeeded. They were married in September of 1931, and moved into an apartment above Anne's parents.

During this period, Joe too became enamoured. He met Fannie Low at an outing of the Prairie Club, a Chicago-area hiking club. Fannie wanted to learn about sports, something in which she had never taken part. It was new, different and likely, from her perspective, a little rebellious. So Joe accommodated Fannie, teaching her to ski, skate and climb. They were married in 1930.

The marriage did not work out very well. As Joe remembers:

"We were married for two years. I didn't have many happy times. Fannie was from a Jewish family. One of her brothers was a psychiatrist. The other had a business. But I was just a common working man. Fannie's sister thought I was no good because I did sports. Her family felt I wasn't aggressive enough. They either thought that I ought to start my own business or they wanted me to get a 'good' job. They wanted me to be a 'Jewish' businessman. We never fitted together. They were concerned with money and status. But I wanted to live.

"In many ways I was too young to settle down. I worked, and I took vacations to go climbing and skiing. I liked this. I think this bothered Fannie and her family. To make matters worse, Fannie's sister got divorced, and she seemed to want to break up our marriage, too.

"I took Fannie to Colorado. She rode in a side car attached to my motorcycle. We visited Longs Peak and climbed Alexanders Chimney. Later, we went to Winter Park and climbed Sheeps Mountain near Berthoud Pass. Fannie thought she had to do the same things as Anne. But I don't think she really enjoyed it. She did like to hike and walk, though.

"During the winter I taught Fannie how to skate. In spite of all this, we weren't very happy. We got divorced in 1932. I was hurt by this, but got over it within several weeks. I don't think any real love had developed between Fannie and me. I was young and human. It was probably a mistake to marry Fannie. Several years later, in 1936, she made an effort to reconcile, but that didn't work out.

"During the summer of my divorce, I wanted to go into the mountains. I needed to go to the mountains. In a way, I would have liked Paul to go with me. But when he was married, Anne said, 'Paul, no more motorcycles.' So he gave up motorcycling and his motorcycle. At the same time, I wanted to be alone. So I didn't ask him. I was alone again. I didn't have anybody.

"I drove my motorcycle to Colorado, to the Indian Peaks area. I parked my motorcycle and set up my pup tent near Brainard Lake or Long Lake.

"The next day I climbed around the ridge and the cirque there. I think I climbed Toll, Shoshoni, Navajo and Apache Peaks. I did all the peaks on the cirque. I was by myself, so I guess they were solo climbs. But they were easy climbs. Up and down all these mountains in one day. It was dark when I returned. I remember wandering into a swamp in the dark in my effort to find my motorcycle and tent. Eventually I found them."

Upon returning to Chicago, Joe made an effort to resume a bachelor's life. In addition to carousing around, he taught Naturfreunde and coworkers how to ski at Wilmot ski area, much to the annoyance of ski instructors there who thought he ought to charge a fee. With friends, he took ski trips to Colorado and elsewhere.

On one of these trips in early spring, Joe and several friends from

Naturefreunde went backcountry skiing near the Berthoud Pass in Colorado. The weather was gorgeous, and the sun beamed its warmth on the upper snowfields. Someone reasoned that it was an ideal day to ski naked. Another had a camera and snapped several shots of the skiers *au naturel*, including one of Joe standing Adonis-like on a rock. Apparently less than proud of the photo, Joe hid it in a drawer in his apartment in Chicago. A couple of years later, in preparation for a trip, he asked two female friends to look after his apartment during his absence. Not only did they look after it, they also looked through it and found the photo. They had it enlarged to near life-size and hung it prominently on the wall in his living room. When Joe arrived home, he was mortified. In 1995, in preparation for his move to Laramie, Joe discovered the original print among his belongings and thought it best destroyed. But his daughter Ginni intervened, prevented an impulsive act and rescued the photo.

In spite of such fun and games, Joe also dreamed of climbing again with Paul. Plans were made for the next summer.

"In August of 1933," Joe continued, "Paul and I went back to Colorado with six other people who were members of the Naturfreunde. Our goal was to climb Longs Peak. We had all hiked up to the Boulderfield Cabin the day before. We started out at about 8:00 a.m. and started hiking up the Cable Trail to the North Face. Soon, however, we decided to split up. Six of us took the Cable Route, while Paul and I went off by ourselves. We wanted to try a different and more interesting route.

"There are several chimneys between the Keyhole and the Cable Trail. We climbed over the boulders to the snowfield below the big wall between the Keyhole and the chimney we intended to climb. We reached the wall, climbing across the snowbank and up over steep ledges to the left until we reached the upper snowfield. We kept climbing around to the right of the snowfield until we were high enough to cross over to the pinnacle, which later continued on as a chimney.

On the North Face of Longs Peak.

"We climbed straight up to a small snow spot, which was the highest snow point at that time. There, the real chimney started, and we climbed walls that were relatively smooth to approximately 300 feet below the notch. We swung out to the right on the open wall and, climbing on ledges, followed up to the ridge. We continued over notches and pinnacles up to the top of Longs Peak, where we met the other members of our party. Later that day, we took the usual Keyhole Trail down to the Boulderfield.

"Our climb was short and not extremely complicated, but very interesting. I recommend this climb, as I liked this route better than any, with the exception of the East Face. I think this was probably a new route, although there were guides who stayed on the Boulderfield and may have done it."

It is difficult to determine the exact location of Joe and Paul's route. It appears that they began at the upper northern part (The Dovetail) of the snowfield known as The Dove on the North Face of Longs. From there nearly straight up, there are several pinnacles. In Richard DuMais' guide book *The High Peaks: A Climbing Guide to the Mountains of Rocky Mountain National Park*, there is a route (No. 117) that traverses left from the highest snow patch. It appears that, rather than traversing, Joe and Paul climbed straight up from the point of traverse to reach a point on the summit ridge north of the pinnacles. There is no record of this route having been climbed previously or repeated.

During the 1933 trip, Joe and Paul had other adventures in mind. According to Joe:

"Paul and I also got away to attempt Lindberg Peak, which is just south of Rocky Mountain National Park. Now the peak is called Lone Eagle Peak. Lone Eagle sounds like an Indian name, and that is a good name for a peak in the Indian Peaks. But, as I understand, its name came from Charles Lindberg's nickname, which he acquired during his solo flight across the Alantic.

"Lone Eagle is really a ridge that runs off a mountain — Apache Peak, maybe. From the North, at Crater Lake, Lone Eagle Peak is a very dramatic spire. Paul and I climbed it."

Seven years later in 1940, a group from the Colorado Mountain Club climbed the north face of Lone Eagle. When close to the top, they reached a very difficult section, which, as it turned out, was the crux pitch of Joe and Paul's climb of the north face. The group's leader, Roy Murchison, elected to traverse around, and reached the summit via an easier route. Group members Bob Ormes and Elwyn Arps, however, remained below this difficult section. From a small platform near the top, Murchison dropped a rope down the crux pitch to Ormes and Arps, who, *(right) "Lone Eagle is really a ridge that runs off a mountain — Apache Peak, maybe." Actually Lone Eagle [center] runs off Mt. George, Apache Peak is on the left.*

(below) The north face of Lone Eagle Peak, showing the approximate route of the Stettners' climb. (Courtesy the Colorado Mountain Club)

*Paul leading on
Lone Eagle Peak
in 1933.*

with the security of a top rope, ascended the crack led by Paul Stettner seven years earlier.

Assuming that they had made the first ascent, Ormes wrote about the climb in the September 1940 edition of the Colorado Mountain Club's *Trail and Timberline* magazine:

> There are several reasons for ranking this climb among the very best in the state: the rock is not surpassed anywhere for firmness and dependability; the ascent has considerable technical variety; it has quantity of climbing; its climax, like that of Ellingwood Arete on Crestone Needle, is at the top where it should be; and while it is not at all a dangerous climb for people of the right experience, it is undeniably a thriller of the first rank.

Jack Fralick, friend of Joe and Paul, read the *Trail and Timberline* article and wrote to Ormes; that he believed that the Stettner brothers had climbed the route seven years before. In the November 1941 issue of *Trial and Timberline*, Bob Ormes corrected his earlier claim. Here is his article, which includes portions of Fralick's letter describing the Stettner brothers' route:

> Last year's North Face climb of Lone Eagle Peak, led by Roy Murchinson and reported by me in *Trail and Timberline*, and later in the *American Alpine Journal*, has brought to light a very interesting letter from John F. Fralick, president of the Chicago Mountaineering Club and also a C.M.C. member.
>
> I had been unable to learn of any previous successes on the North face of the Peak, and so prematurely assumed that our climb was a first. Fralick discussed the matter with the brothers Paul and Joseph Stettner, who pioneered the Stettner Ledges climb on the East Face of Longs, and he learned that they had done the Lone Eagle face on August 30, 1933.

The Stettners took to the rocks where the C.M.C. party did, and then continued more directly on the north face instead of following the ledge around to the west and doing the easier trough climb there.

From the broad grass ledge where we had lunch, they climbed a crack to the bridge of the nose. Fralick reports that this section "formed the principal difficulty of the ascent. The crack, the upper part of which is visible at the bottom of the picture, overhangs and presents a pitch of the greatest difficulty, probably more severe than any step on the Stettners Ledges. . . . Paul Stettner is of the opinion that this crack is the most southerly of the fissures in the north end of the west flank of the peak that can be climbed. Your (our) corner climb was apparently made closer to the extreme north end of the west flank. Both routes seem to meet on the bridge of the nose . . .

The Stettners left Crater Lake at 1:30 p.m., and were seen near the top, by companions who had remained at the lake, at about 3:30 p.m. They descended the East Face (as did Elwyn Arps with one or two of the Juniors) and returned to camp at Monarch Lake at 9:30 that night.

After studying the photographs kindly furnished by the Stettners, I believe their crack, which is apparently formed by the right hand edge of a flake, must have been the one which Arps and I took by way of variation from the shorter piton traverse by which Murchison led the rest of our party into the easier, upper section of the corner climb. We found the crack section of 40 or 50 feet extremely strenuous, even with the security of the rope lowered from Roy's platform. To the best of my knowledge there could have been no other feasible route to the nose bridge than these two, unless one climbed considerably farther around on the west face and then returned to the nose bridge on a horizontal ledge.

May we offer belated congratulations to the Stettners for the imagination and skill they showed in pioneering this splendid rock climb.

Paul on the summit ridge of Lone Eagle Peak.

Joe and Paul had once again neglected to publicize their climb. Fralick had learned about it through casual conversations with Joe and Paul. Again, why the modesty?

During this period, Joe and Paul were actively involved in the German-American community of Chicago. They may have felt little need to tell of their mountaineering exploits outside this relatively small German-speaking community. But the more likely explanation comes from their friend and climbing companion Jack Fralick, who offers this explanation in an article from *Climbing*:[10]

> The Stettner approach to climbing was spontaneous and lighthearted. They climbed primarily for the pure joy of the sport and out of their love for the mountain environment. Records and fame meant nothing to them . . . The mountains provided fun and adventure to the Stettners and all who went with them.

Over 60 years have elapsed, so perhaps Joe's recollection of his own feelings and motives for not seeking publicity are not totally accurate. Nonetheless, here is his explanation:

"All climbing should be fun. Paul and I wanted to do different climbs. New climbs gave us fun and adventure. But once the climb was over, it was over. We didn't make much of a fuss about it. There was no reason to. Climbing is different now. It has changed. But we never really talked about these climbs. If others wanted to do the climb, Paul and I were always ready to talk about it.

"I did keep notes about our climbs, often in German. I never thought about publishing them. When I was young and a member of the Sektion Neuland of the German-Austrian Alpine Club, we were required to keep a record of our climbs. I did it then and continued the habit. I was better at this than Paul. I'm glad I kept the notes. So if you want to do one of our climbs, I can still tell you about it."

chapter 9

Joe's Solo

The summer of 1936 was one of charged emotion for Joe. Although his marriage had ended several years before, his former wife Fannie had attempted a reconciliation. The effort was not successful, and she disappeared from his life. Paul's marriage, in contrast, was faring well. Joe recollects some of the more immediate circumstances surrounding his trip to Longs Peak that summer:

"Paul and several of his friends from a gymnastics club in Chicago, who were good hikers and gymnasts, went to the Tetons. I had agreed to go to Colorado with two married couples. We all belonged to the Naturfreunde. There were five of us, including me. One of the couples didn't get along very well. There was a significant age difference between the man and the woman, and they were always arguing with one another. She was unhappy. He showed no emotion toward her. The man was an old friend, and I wanted to help them but didn't know how to. I couldn't do anything for them. This frustrated me. The other couple was much younger. They were on their honeymoon and seemed to be very happy together and preoccupied with each other. It all seemed to upset me."

At an earlier time Joe recorded some memories about that trip. These notes are sprinkled with several recent comments he has made about his emotional state at the time and about the climb. "Our plan was to climb the North Face of Longs Peak. We hiked up to the timberline and stayed at the shelter house there. The next day, only three of us actually attempted the climb. The young couple stayed behind. And, of those, only my old friend accompanied me to the top. That evening, we returned to our camp near the timberline.

"The whole scene was bothering me. During the climb, I kept on having this feeling that I wanted to be out alone, to be alone with nature. There were other things on my mind. My marriage was over. I didn't really want to go back. I kept on thinking that maybe I was not as good a climber as others thought I was. And I was worried about what the others were thinking about me. I was really very blue.

"I decided that, the next day, I would solo climb the East Face of Longs to the southeast point. That's right south of the big notch. I didn't think it had been climbed before, and I wanted to be one of those who made this climb.

"But that was only part of it. As I said, I was kind of blue. I had to let something out of my mind. I felt I had to do some thinking. It wasn't that I had to do something special. But I did want to be alone, and I felt I had to do this for myself. In some ways, I don't really know why I felt I had to do it. It was my birthday, September 8, 1936.

"The next morning, I started out at 5:00 a.m. and made my way to Chasm Lake. I climbed up the left ridge until I reached the upper glacier. I climbed it to the bottom of Alexanders Chimney. There, I changed my hobnailed boots for climbing shoes.

"I had approximately six pitons, my climbing hammer, about 15 feet of light rope and a sandwich. My heavy boots, I left at the base of Alexanders Chimney. It was not a difficult climb up Alexanders Chimney, and I made very good time up to Broadway. As I reached Broadway, I crossed the ledge to the big couloir between the main peak and the southeast peak. Then I started up the chimneys which were from 50 to 100 feet high. During this time I had the feeling that nothing was going to hurt me. Yet, I really didn't care if I fell and got hurt. I knew that this climb would make me feel better.

"Most of the time I kept as close as possible to the ridge facing the gully. Soon after that I had to climb on quite an exposed wall up the ridge, which extended to the top. I climbed up this ridge to within 200 and 300 feet of the top.

"About that time, I found myself in a complicated spot. I needed two or three more pitons, but I had only one left. I tried to get over the difficult spot, but I found it impossible to make this climb. I went back down about 100 feet, then to the left, where I found a fairly good route through a crevice. Then I went on up until I reached the top.

"In the meantime, it had started to rain, then sleet, hail and snow. There was also a lot of thunder and lightning. When I reached the top, at about 11:00 a.m., I was actually in the clouds. The climb took me about six hours. It was cold, and I was very uncomfortable and, therefore, didn't stay up there long.

"I had a complicated trip down, mainly due to the bad weather. I followed the south ridge over to the upper part of Mills Glacier, which connects the top with the lower glacier. The falling rain and ice made the trip dangerous. I kept to the right on the shoulder east of the glacier. About 300 feet down on the shoulder, I was forced to cross the glacier, which was steep and icy. Due to the fact that I was wearing climbing shoes, I was forced to chop foot and hand grips with my climbing hammer into the clear ice. I finally reached the shoulder on the other side of the glacier. From there I continued down to the base of Alexanders Chimney. I had to inch my way down. There I found my boots again and put them on. The rest of the way down the glacier was simple, as I actually slid down most of the way to Chasm Lake.

"Soon after that I was in the shelter cabin at Chasm Lake, where my friends were waiting for me. They had a snack ready, and we celebrated. I felt I had completed a successful trip in many ways."

This climb, which later became known as "Joe's Solo", has been surrounded with controversy. There has been controversy about the route itself, and there has been controversy about the wisdom of solo climbing in the first place.

Concerning the route, Walter Fricke wrote in his *Climber's Guidebook to Rocky Mountain National Park*:

> Gorrell's photograph showed the route ascending the right edge of this headwall, and Nesbit followed suit after corresponding with Joe Stettner, who thought the line was correct. Close inspection from several angles suggests the unlikelihood, however, of any unbelayed solo route continuing in this line, although no one had given it a real try recently.

Fricke's skepticism seems to have arisen from three concerns: the degree of difficulty, his disbelief that anyone would have tried the route without a rope and belay and the fact that no one had repeated the route.

Bob Godfrey and Dudley Chelton contributed a paragraph of their book *Climb!* to this discussion:

> This ascent has been much discussed during subsequent years. Warren Gorrell had a photograph of the East Face showing the line of Joe's solo ascent. Stettner examined the photograph in later years and felt that the line was correct. Modern climbers who have explored this region of the East Face have returned

impressed with its steepness and difficulty. Walter Fricke, in his climbers guidebook writes, 'Close inspection from several angles suggests the unlikelihood . . . of an unbelayed solo route continuing in this line.' Joe Stettner remains convinced that the line shown in Gorrell's photograph is correct and that he cut left only about a hundred feet from the top. In his words, he found the upper part 'very hard and felt that I took chances on it.' In retrospect, it is impossible to ascertain with complete certainty the exact nature and line of Joe Stettner's solo climb. It is possible he was mistaken on examining Gorrell's photographs, and that his actual line of ascent was further left on more broken and easier ground. However, there is no doubt that he was climbing at a high technical standard during the 1930's. It is quite possible that, in the excitement of finding himself alone on that great face, all of his energies, spurred on by the unthinkable consequences of an unroped fall, motivated him to follow the difficult line indicated on Gorrell's photographs.

Jim Peavler, in his writings on the Stettners, also contributes several thoughts to this discussion. At the time of the climb, Joe was perhaps more familiar with the East Face than anyone. He had studied maps and photographs of the East Face and had climbed there several times, including the Stettner Ledges just below Joe's Solo. Peavler also suggests that Joe had no motive to deliberately misrepresent the climb because he and Paul had never displayed any interest in publicizing their climbs in the first place. And they did like to explore new routes. Peavler notes that Joe was disturbed by personal matters and left the camp that morning with a desire to do something that would absorb his consciousness totally. And he states that "the man who climbed Joe's Solo was one of the world's most skilled mountain climbers and was a man possessed."

Richard DuMais in his guidebook shows Joe's Solo veering far to the left about two-thirds of the way to the top of the great pillar. Thus DuMais seems to have accepted Walter Fricke's explanation and description of Joe's route; although in his verbal route description, DuMais wrote that one can "either traverse left from here to reach the 8th Route (where Fricke thought Joe climbed) or head up near the right edge of the headwall above to reach the top of the ridge (where Joe believes his route went.)"

No effort is made here to resolve this controversy. Nonetheless Michael Covington's experiences on the East Face of Longs in the late 1970s may cast some new light on the matter. Covington is a well-known climber, and was director of the Fantasy Ridge guide service in Estes Park during the 1970s and early 1980s. While climbing in 1977, in the vicinity of the purported route of Joe's Solo, Covington found himself on a rather difficult section, which he estimated to be in the 5.8 to 5.9 range. He found an old piton driven into a crack. He had no idea where it came from. Upon completing the route, he and his partner Duncan Ferguson named the route "Teeter-Totter Pillar."

During a conversation with Covington several months later, he asked me if, to the best of my knowledge, Joe Stettner had left a piton up there. I, of course, did not know the answer.

The next time I saw Joe I asked him. He told me that on a particular blank section he hammered in a piton, hung a sling and rested a while. Then he used it as a hand hold and was able to extricate himself from this difficult spot. He couldn't extract several of his pitons, so he left them there.

Joe's presence in the vicinity of Covington's Teeter-Totter Pillar route seems to be the only explanation for this old piton. Perhaps this is a little like the old "watch on the beach" — proof for the existence of God — which if persuasive enough proof in theology, then a piton on the East Face ought to be convincing proof for Joe's Solo in mountaineering history.

Concerning solo climbing, Fricke impliedly asks: why would anyone go there without the protection of a rope and belay? Joe himself remembers the climb being "very hard" and concedes that he "took chances on it." This exchange raises the current issue of free soloing, an aspect of climbing that seems to be increasingly popular today.

Sixty years after Joe's Solo, Joe was standing in his kitchen scrambling eggs for breakfast. Between mutters about his increasing lack of dexterity, and the nuisance of the small bits of egg shell he was getting in his morning's work, Joe remarked, "I can understand why climbers like Derek Hersey[11] do solo climbing. I didn't do it very often. Usually Paul and I went together. And Joe's Solo was the hardest one I ever did. But I understand. You are there by yourself. There is more excitement if you are alone. There is no protection. You have to rely on your own judgment — no one to discuss the next steps with. So you become totally involved in the next move. It is fundamental.

"I remember on Joe's Solo, when I came to a very difficult part, I put in a piton and tied the rope to it. Then I would climb above that place and put a new piton in and tie myself to it. I would then climb back down and untie the rope and try to remove the piton. It was a form of self-belay. So I tried to make it as safe as possible. I know it was risky, but I understand why climbers do it. On the other hand, I never thought about getting myself into real danger.

"And on that climb I wanted to get rid of my feelings — make a 'clean slate.' You want to prove something to yourself. The nature of it requires that you get rid of all other worries. I was letting off steam, being totally alone. And I was kind of aimless. I had no idea about the future.

"The idea of making a name for myself never came into my mind. Neither Paul nor I ever thought about becoming famous. Walter Fricke was wrong. I never thought of doing a climb that others could not do or to make a name for myself.

"Too many young climbers solo to make a name for themselves. Probably 75 percent do so to make themselves known. You know, many people will do almost anything to get their name in the paper — even kill themselves. Soloing almost has become competitive. It's become like bouldering. And that's different.

"This is what I would say to young climbers. If you solo for the enjoyment of it, why not? Do it to let the pressure off, as I did on Joe's Solo. Do it because you trust yourself. Do the climb and don't destroy yourself. Don't do it for the name. Don't do it for the fame."

There is evidence that Joe's attitude toward soloing has not been totally consistent. In 1949, Joe, Paul, Jack Fralick, Joe Hawkes and Harry Lumby wrote the *Chicago Mountaineering Club Safety Manual*, a 14-page booklet that covered many aspects of climbing, including rope technique, snow and ice technique, bivouacs, belaying, map and compass use and first aid. In the section entitled "Roping Up," the first principle is: "No solo climbs! It is entirely too dangerous." Five years later in a Club safety report, Joe and Lothar Kolbig wrote: "Solo completely discouraged." I never had the opportunity to confront Joe with this inconsistency. Perhaps he was simply out-voted.

The year 1936 was significant for several reasons. Joe brought his mother to the States for a visit. They had not seen each other for eleven years. It was a wonderful reunion for Mother Stettner, Joe and Paul. But she also sensed the worst was in store for them. She predicted that, "This is the last time I am going to see you." The Nazis had just closed the borders, making future travel and visits virtually impossible. All future mail would have to go through Italy. It was a foreshadow of what was to come.

The year also brought an end to Joe's "iron horse." On the assumption that Mother Stettner would be less than enthusiastic about touring the country on his motorcycle or in its side car, Joe traded in the trusty steed for a "wheel barrow," as he once referred to the four-wheeled means of transportation that once indirectly challenged Paul and him. Thus, forever went his beloved means of getting to the mountains, and his source of adventure and numerous spills.

chapter *10*

On to the Tetons

I n 1936 and 1937, the Stettners extended their mountaineering beyond Colorado and into Wyoming. In September 1936, Paul visited the Tetons with friends. He climbed the southeast side of the Grand Teton with Arthur Lehnebach, with whom he had done some practice climbs at Devils Lake in Wisconsin. They were the second party to ascend, and the first to descend, the Petzoldt-Loomis-Otterbody route.

By coincidence, Walter Kiener also was climbing in the Tetons. He noticed the Stettner name in the camp register, looked up Paul and introduced him to several well-known climbers, including Paul Petzoldt, Fritiof Fryxell, Warren Gorrell and Fritz Wiessner. Wiessner had just led the second ascent of the North Ridge of the Grand Teton. He and his climbing partners were very enthusiastic about the route and encouraged Paul to do it. Paul wanted to wait until the next summer when Joe could climb it with him.

Joe remembers that, "In September of 1937, Paul and I drove to the Tetons together. When we discussed our plans at the Park Headquarters, they strongly discouraged us from climbing the North Ridge of the Grand Teton this late in the season. Jack Durrance felt strongly about this. But we had already made up our minds and went up to Amphitheater Lake and set up camp.

"At the lake we felt it would be wise to have a good look at the North Ridge before attempting to climb it. For this reason, we decided to climb Mt. Owen first. This we did on September 7th. It was icy in spots,

At Jenny Lake in 1937 with (right to left) Anne Stettner, Paul Petzoldt, Walter Kiener, Warren Gorrell, unidentified, Jack Durrance, and unidentified.

but we made it without any problems. It was a nice climb. We hiked up the Teton Glacier and past the Koven Couloir and ascended the south east face up to the second snow bench. From there we went along the snow to a point where we could climb to the summit. It's hard to say exactly where we went. I'm uncertain. Paul and I wanted to study the North Ridge of the Grand. We picked our way with this in mind. We didn't take an established route. We just climbed and studied the North Ridge. We got a good look at it."

During Joe's story of that reconnaissance climb he failed to mention that, in the process, he and Paul did the first ascent of the nose variation of the East Ridge of Mount Owen, a climb that is rated Grade III, 5.6, A-1 in Ortenburger and Jackson's *A Climber's Guide To The Teton Range.*

Joe continued, "The next day Paul and I hiked to the Middle Teton, up through the South Fork of Garnet Canyon. We climbed up the dike to the summit. I'd call it a 'medium' climb — not too hard and not too exciting." It was likely the first ascent of the entire Dike Route, rated today as 5.5.

(Above) Joe on the East Ridge of Mount Owen in 1937.
(Below) Joe signs into the summit register of Mount Owen.

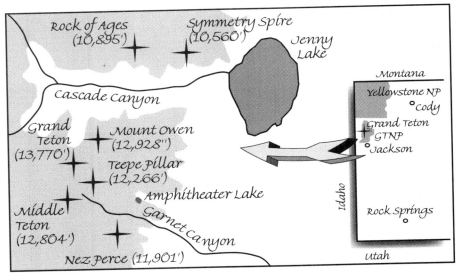

A map showing many of the Stettners' climbs in Wyoming's Teton Range.

"On 10th of September, Paul and I set out to climb the North Ridge of the Grand Teton. Starting from Amphitheater Lake, we crossed Teton Glacier and walked to the foot of the Gunsight Notch between the Grand and Mt. Owen. There we climbed halfway up the wall they call The Grandstand. It was not too hard, but as it got more difficult, we roped up. Paul took the lead, and I carried the pack with our gear. I belayed him while he went up about 30 feet. Then I followed him.

"At one place, I felt rather off balance, and I called to Paul to tell him that I might slip. 'It's OK,' he yelled back. At that moment, I lost my footing and swung away from the wall. But fortunately, I swung back to the wall and continued to climb up to Paul. After a few rope lengths, we got up to the shoulder of The Grandstand, which already is close to the chimney that leads to the ridge and the summit.

"The back of the chimney was packed with snow. From here, it was my turn to lead, and for Paul to haul the pack. I climbed in the snow up to my knees. As I looked down on Paul, I wondered for a second how he would hold me if I were to slip and come down with all that snow. I went 30 to 40 feet, stopped and belayed Paul as he climbed up to me.

"We repeated this routine several times, until we got to the overhanging chockstone. Here, I told Paul that I had had enough and that he had better take over the lead. Paul tried several ways to climb the chockstone and eventually made it. There was a rope hanging there, over the chockstone, that Paul Petzoldt had left in August when he was climbing the route. Because we did not trust it, we did not use it. After Paul pulled up our knapsack, I managed to climb the chockstone, too. Although I had a good belay, it was still difficult.

"The chimney above was relatively easy after the chockstone. We continued upward until we got to a big wall and had to traverse it. This brought us to an open, smooth plate. Under ordinary conditions, this would have been relatively easy to cross. But this time, it was covered with a thin sheet of ice. It was impossible to cross without chopping holds with our climbing hammer. I climbed up a little higher along on the side and placed a piton and a carabiner, through which I put the rope. I was then able to give Paul a good belay. Slowly he chopped holds in the ice and carefully crossed over the icy plate. Once on the other side, he found a good spot to belay me.

"I retrieved my piton and carabiner and followed him. Once over this tricky spot, we made good progress and, in a few rope lengths, were on the summit.

"It was getting late. At 7:10 p.m., we signed in the summit register and sat down for a few minutes. The sun was going down fast on the horizon, so we decided to bivouac on the top. After exploring a little, we found a suitable spot, where we ate what food we had left, sat on our ropes and put our feet in the knapsack.

The North Face of the Grand Teton showing various routes, with the North Ridge route on the right skyline. The Becky Couloir route (the true "Stettner Couloir") goes down behind the snowfield to the left of the summit.

*Paul (at left) and Joe at the time of their last big
climb together on the Grand Teton in 1937.*

"The view of Jenny Lake was beautiful. Gradually it got dark, the
cars put on their lights, and the houses lit up in the valley. The night was
clear. The bright stars emerged and sparkled brilliantly. It was such a
beautiful sight. We talked over the many climbs we had done together,
about the friends we had in Chicago and wondered what they would think
if they knew where we were now. Finally we dozed off.

"We didn't know it at the time, but this was the last really big
climb that Paul and I would make together. It was our last big summit.
We did other climbs, but nothing like this. We had been climbing
partners for nearly 20 years. Circumstances gradually took us in different
directions. There was the war. Paul did a lot of guiding for the Iowa
Mountaineers. His family took on increasing importance. Paul Jr., was
born. And then we both became involved with the Chicago
Mountaineering Club. We went on CMC outings together, but we were
always leaders, went separate ways and to different places with our own
groups.

"We didn't know this was going to happen when we climbed the
North Ridge. Do you know, Jack, Paul was a better climber than I was.
I never told anyone that before. And I never told Paul. Perhaps I should
have told him then."

Joe's view was not universally shared. When I related Joe's comment to older CMC member Rod Harris, Rod reported that this was not the consensus among Club members. Although there is little point in adding to a senseless debate, I do so anyway: I suspect that Paul was the better rock gymnast, and this greatly impressed Joe. On the other hand, Joe was a great rock climber and had equally great mountaineering sense. This impressed club members. Their respective strengths complemented each other. It was this combination of gymnastics, boldness, caution and great mountaineering sense that made the Stettner brothers one of the great climbing teams of all time.

"I don't know how much we slept that night on the summit of the Grand," Joe continued, "but soon we were waiting for the sun to rise. Eventually the sky turned red, and we decided to start down. With some climbing and lots of rappelling, we aimed in the direction of Teepes Pillar.

"When we got down to the bottom of the wall, we climbed along it and descended a snow couloir. We stayed along the wall so that we could get down to our tent at the lake. When we got down the snow, Paul suggested that, since we came down that snow, we should go back up. Paul's idea wasn't bad, but we were tired. So we came back, a couple of years later, and climbed it.[12] I think that is how it got the name 'Stettner Couloir.'

"Once we passed Teepes, we aimed directly toward our tent on Amphitheater Lake. It was noon when we got there. We took a short dip in the lake and turned to rest for the remaining part of the day. We considered our climb to be very successful."

The Stettners frequently selected the month of September for their trips to the mountains, a time that many considered to be too late in the climbing season. There are several explanations for attempting these climbs so late in the year. In Europe, September often brings warm and stable weather, and it seems that the Stettners were in the habit of climbing during that month. Also, vacation time, and the need to earn a little more money, may have played a role. But most importantly, they felt confident that they could climb alpine routes in September and were, perhaps, a bit stubborn.

Joe seemed almost unaware of the confusion that has surrounded the Grand Teton climb. Teton historians are convinced that the route Joe and Paul descended in 1937, and later ascended in 1941, is known as the "Beckey Couloir." Fred Beckey, Graham Matthews and Ralph Widrig climbed the route in 1948, and thought it was a first ascent. Thus, the actual Stettner route acquired its name Beckey Couloir. Another couloir, one couloir to the east of the Beckey Couloir, acquired the name "Stettner Couloir," even though Joe and Paul never climbed that route.

The Grand Teton from the south. The arrow on the left points
toward the Stettner descent route (the true Stettner Couloir) while
the arrow on the right marks the mis-named "Stettner Couloir."

Younger and Strube first descended it in 1933, and Schaeffer, Fielding and Stout first ascended it in 1964. Over the years, climbers mistakenly referred to the Younger-Strube route as "Stettners Couloir" and the Stettner route as the "Beckey Couloir," thereby firmly entrenching these names in Teton lore. In spite of historical inaccuracies, Ortenburger and Jackson in their guide book, and the National Park Service in the Tetons, have elected to keep matters as they are — continuity in terminology apparently being of greater importance than historical accuracy. This confusion was caused by Joe and Paul's habit of doing a route for the pure joy of it, packing up and going home without making a fuss about it and, in some cases, without even mentioning it.

Nonetheless, their new route on the Grand Teton attracted attention. In *Climbing in North America*, Chris Jones wrote:

> As with the rest of their early climbs, this new route on the
> Grand Teton went unrecorded. Recognition of their achievement
> had to wait the researches of later climbers. If this talented pair
> had enjoyed the leisure time of other climbers of the day, who
> were mostly well to do, their contribution would have been even
> more significant.

It was Jack Fralick[13] who brought most of the Stettner climbs, including this one, to the climbing world's attention. He reported that the brothers were apparently unaware of the normal Owen Route off the mountain, so they just headed straight down the south face into Garnett Canyon to get to their camp and tent. Fralick added that this was a "rare descent of the Grand by a line other than the Owen Route and, considering the reputation of the North Ridge and the prevailing conditions, this traverse of the Grand Teton was a most audacious undertaking."

Joe, at 94, seemed amused by Fralick's claim. "Later, Jack Fralick claimed that the Stettners climbed the couloir first. He is always saying something like that. I really don't know if that is true or not. But it really doesn't make any difference. Names and numbers never meant much to me. I wanted the rock. If it had hand holds and it worked, then I wanted it."

chapter *11*

Birth of a club

*U*niversity laboratories, as all men know, are dedicated to scientific research and learning. This is especially true at the University of Chicago, where more Nobel Prize-winning laureates have found their academic home than in any other university in the world. It must have been particularly disturbing to have found three students of that renowned spot of academe reveling in mountaineering sagas and dreams, when they ought to have been engaging in scientific measurement and the pursuit of truth as understood by scientists.

Harold and Bill Plumley and Jack Fralicks' dreams were not idle. In the past, their fantasies had won the name of action. Our three young, distracted scientists already had experienced the mountains. Harold and his younger brother Bill had experimented with climbing before their arrival at the university. In 1934, Harold and Bill visited the Tetons, where they retained the services of Paul Petzoldt, well-known Teton guide, who schooled them in the art of climbing and in the sagas of Teton mountaineering.

Jack Fralick first travelled to the mountains with his family in 1935 at the age of 16. The highlight of the trip was a journey on horseback and on foot to Chasm Lake in Rocky Mountain National Park. As they scanned the awesome cliffs of the East Face of Longs Peak, high above the lake, they were fascinated to see a solitary climber make his way down the snowfield at the foot of the wall. When the climber arrived at the lake, they pestered him with a barrage of questions. He was Warren Gorrell, also from Chicago. He had been "tinkering around Stettner Ledges." Gorrell said that only he, Charlie Hewes and climbing guide Walter Kiener knew about the Stettner route. He wanted to repeat it. And he did, making the second ascent of the Ledges, with three other climbers, the following summer.

In 1937, Fralick returned and climbed Kieners Route on the East Face of Longs Peak with Gorrell and Walter Kiener. During the climb, he heard a lot more about the Stettners. "I'd go anywhere with the Stettners," Kiener said. Gorrell suggested that the Stettners lived in Chicago, but he did not know how to locate them.

Fralick first made it to the Tetons in 1936. He too climbed with Petzoldt, who again spun tales of great climbs and great climbers. Petzoldt informed Jack that two young climbers, the Plumley brothers, were in Oak Park and attended the University of Chicago. Upon entering U of C in 1937, Jack kept an eye open for Bill, who belonged to a fraternity housed next door to his own.

By the fall of 1937, Bill Plumley and Jack Fralick had found one another. They located Harold and met together in a physics laboratory, where the joy of telling mountaineering tales exceeded their commitment to scientific inquiry. Their imaginations ran wild. Harold became George Mallory of Everest fame; Bill became the Italian guide Jean-Antoine Carrel; and Jack became A.F. Mummery, who disappeared on Nanga Parbat (26,658 ft.) in 1895. Mummery was also eloquent, having written words that expressed Jack's feelings about mountains, "At the age of 19, the crags of the Via Mala and the snows of the Theodule cast a spell over me which to no small extent determined the course of my life." Our young climbers began to refer to one another by the names of their adopted heroes.

They resolved to visit the Tetons together in the late spring of the next year. When the academic year ended, they headed for Wyoming.[14]

Although full of resolve, their ambitions were thwarted by too much snow and severe storms, conditions that tamed their sharp sense of adventure. During one storm, the clouds broke momentarily, offering a glimpse of the full height of Mount Owen. It glistened with snow and ice from top to bottom. The view enthralled and intimidated them. Forsaking the high peaks of the Teton Range, they headed for a pinnacle high on the East Ridge of Symmetry Spire, which stands at 10,560 feet.

In the tradition of true Midwestern mountaineers, they picked a route that led to impassable overhangs. Eventually, in a display of prudence, they retreated. Nearly forced to bivouac, they made an epic descent to Jenny Lake.

Undaunted, they returned and tried a different route. This time they reached the top of the little pinnacle. They found no indication that anyone had ever been there before, so the young scientists felt entitled to exercise that natural right of all first ascenders — to name their conquest. But what name to give it?

It so happened that these boys, in an effort to maintain the high level of energy demanded by mountaineering, had been observing a strict diet of cube steaks. When they reached the summit, they felt hungry. Eureka! They had found their name. The pinnacle must be named "Cube Point" in honor of the diet that made the climb possible.

Richard Rossiter in his book *Teton Classics* writes, "Cube Point takes its name from a large, angular block that forms the actual summit." Rossiter ought to take greater historical and factual care. Cube Point looks more like a pyramid than a cube. Moreover, cubes are not "angular blocks," a reality that gives credence to the Fralick-Plumley claim.

It is appropriate to note that Mummery did not reach the summit of Nanga Parbat, Mallory failed on Everest and Whymper beat Carrel to the summit of the Matterhorn. Thus, they were never empowered to name a peak or even a route.[15] Not so for the Plumleys and Fralick, who at this early moment in their climbing careers, gained a power forever out of reach of their heroes. And they exercised it by naming their peak after a beaten-up piece of meat.

When our scholars returned to the University of Chicago campus for the 1938 fall-semester, they were charged with enthusiasm

1940

(above) *The crest of the Chicago Mountaineering Club, designed by Paul.*

(right) *A 1941 CMC outing at Devils Lake. Paul is holding the child in the back row.*

for more mountaineering and less science. Once again art and affairs of the heart won out.

Fralick ran into Bill Plumley again on the campus in February of 1940. The boys were now in their twenties. Bill suggested the need for a mountaineering club of local climbers, an idea that appealed immediately to Fralick. They sought counsel of Harold, now a graduate and a gainfully employed physicist at Commonwealth Edison. Plans for a club were formulated in the basement of Eckhart Hall. And so, in the laboratories of the University of Chicago — during the same era — both the Chicago Mountaineering Club (CMC) and the nuclear age were born!

Although the Manhattan Project, which conducted the first controlled nuclear reaction, has received more of the world's attention, the CMC has caused the world less trouble. Thus, there is reason to believe that the University of Chicago is equally proud of its two children, both born in the early forties. In 1990, during the CMC's 50th Anniversary Banquet, University of Chicago President Hanna Gray expressed the institution's great pride in Jack, Bill and Harold's contribution to our culture. She wrote:

> The University of Chicago
> Office of the President
>
> Dear Mr. Fralick:
>   I am delighted to send my congratulations to you as you join with the Chicago Mountaineering Club in celebrating its 50th anniversary. As one of the founding members of the Club, you certainly must take special pleasure in contemplating the growth and success of the Club over the past half century.
>   We are delighted by the distinguished accomplishments of our alumni and we're proud of your association with the University.
>   With best wishes on this special occasion,
>
>   Hanna Holborn Gray
>   President

To find members, the CMC founders compiled a list of the names of all Chicago-area climbers they knew about, and wrote to major American and Canadian mountaineering clubs for the names of their members residing in the Chicago area. Although they obtained a number of names, including those of members of the Colorado Mountain Club and the Alpine Club of Canada, the CMC learned nothing of the legendary Stettners' whereabouts. Fralick searched the Chicago phone directory and the "City Directory," which contained the names of every one in Chicago. But he met with no luck.

The first CMC meeting was held at the Union League Club of Chicago on April 24, 1940. Thirty-five people attended. The climbers introduced themselves and shared a little about their climbing experiences, which, in general, were modest. One attendee, Joe Hawkes, said he had done "a little climbing in the West," but failed to mention that it entailed climbing the Grand Teton from Lupine Meadows and descending it in five hours and 22 minutes. In spite of their modesty, several strong climbers emerged from the Chicago area.

The first local outings were organized at a quarry near Lemont, Illinois. "Le mont," as francophiles know, means "the mountain," so it was a most appropriate place for the CMC to begin its adventures. Over the years, CMC members have been plagued by the oft asked question, "Where do you Chicago mountaineers climb? Sears Tower?" The question is always followed with a hearty chuckle. The correct response is, in the best French accent a Chicagoan can muster, "Mon dieu! Non, Monsieur. Nous allons `a da mont."

Although there was no club outing to the West that first year, Bill, Harold and Jack again decided to head for the Tetons, this time bringing Jack's brother Bill along. Bill Fralick lacked a famous climber's pseudonym and suffered from the sense of being excluded from group discourse. The others quickly resolved the problem by bestowing upon him the name "Legendary," standing for the legendary Stettner brothers about whom they had heard so much. Later, while at the Jenny Lake Ranger Station, they scanned the registered climbers list in search of Chicago-area addresses. To their surprise, there were the names of Joe and Paul Stettner, together with their Chicago addresses.

Jack remembers the day when, "upon returning home, I went to Joe's address in Chicago. No one was home. I looked into a window and saw a drawing or picture of a rock wall. I knew then that I had found the Stettners. Next, I headed for Paul's address. He, too, was not home. But his mother-in-law, who lived on the first floor, was. Paul and his wife Anne lived on the second floor of that house. She said that they were at Devils Lake and gave me their telephone number.

"Later I called. Paul answered. I explained that we had formed a mountaineering club and asked if Bill Plumley, his girl friend Donata and I could come over and talk with him about it. There was this very long silence. Finally he said, 'I guess so.' We made arrangements to meet at Paul's house.

"At the meeting, Joe and Paul were cordial enough, but indicated little interest. They were apparently skeptical of the idea of a mountaineering club based in Chicago. After some discussion, we invited them to attend a club outing at the Mississippi Palisades near Savanna, Illinois, where limestone bluffs and spires tower above the Mississippi River. They made no promises or commitments. All they said was, 'We'll see about that.'"

The CMC members arrived early at the Palisades for the outing that fall day and, by midmorning, had climbed several routes up the smooth, weather-polished limestone faces that border the Mississippi River. Fralick had just completed a climb up a vertical wall, and was standing at the top of a bluff, when he noticed a car arrive far below. Two men got out of the car and asked where they could find Jack Fralick. "Up there," some one said, pointing upwards. "He's standing on the top of the bluff." As Fralick remembers, "Joe and Paul put on their rucksacks and started up the vertical wall. They moved gracefully and effortlessly up to where I stood. They floated like a couple of spiders in a style I had never seen before. I had never seen such skill. I knew in an instant that the Stettner legend was real. It was an auspicious moment."

Fralick regards his encouragement of the Stettner brothers to attend the CMC's outing as his most important contribution to the Club's history. "They soon became the real spirit and driving force. They gave us credibility. They were far and above the most important people in the Club."

Bill, Donata and Jack may have persuaded the Stettner brothers to attend the outing, but it is unlikely that they had to persuade the brothers to join the Club. The seeds were already sown. Joe and Paul had been going to Devils Lake with friends of the Naturfreunde for over ten years. These friends enjoyed scrambling about the rocks at the lake, but had little interest in technical climbing. The CMC provided the Stettners with enthusiastic fellow climbers. As Fralick has said, "On some level, they welcomed our invitation."

And so the Stettner brothers became charter members of the Chicago Mountaineering Club. Joe was 39 and Paul, 34. They didn't then realize the impact this choice would have on their lives; they didn't know that it would dramatically change the focus of their climbing. No longer would Joe and Paul search out new and challenging routes to climb. Instead, they were destined to teach, coach and guide generations of Midwestern climbers. And, after joining the Club, they would rarely mountaineer together again.

Another thing they didn't know at the time was that their new friend and climbing partner, Jack Fralick, would make the climbing world aware of what the Stettners had achieved in the mountains.

chapter *12*

Early club Adventures

B y 1941, the enthusiastic, young CMC climbers were on the lookout for good local climbing areas where they could practice climbing and rope handling techniques for future adventures in the mountains of the West. Neither "Le Mont" nor the Mississippi Palisades sufficed. Devils Lake, with its quartzite bluffs and hard routes, offered much more. But the climbs were short, perhaps 50 to 60 feet at most.

Near Camp Douglas in Wisconsin, an hour or so north of Devils Lake, were several high, sandstone towers with multi-pitch climbs. These towers offered exciting, challenging, mountain-like climbing. In the spring of 1941, well-known German-American climber Fritz Wiessner, and a few of his friends, made ascents of some of these towers. On Ragged Towers, a long crack leads to a platform at the junction of the Southeast and Northeast Faces of the highest tower. Wiessner climbed the tower via the Northeast Face, thus avoiding the crack on the Southeast Face that sported a double overhang.

Word of these climbs reached the Chicago climbing community, and in June of 1941, Joe, Paul and Fralick resolved to go to Camp Douglas and take on the challenges of Ragged Towers.

Here is Joe's narrative of this adventure, written the following September:

"There are some places around Chicago where one can get a good workout in mountain climbing. I mean the 'Hard Way,' and we did it.

"Jack Fralick, Paul and I planned a little practice trip up to Camp Douglas, Wisconsin, 260 miles from Chicago. We stopped off at Devils Lake, where we expected to meet other climbers. We used up the 'waiting time' by climbing some of the cliffs on the western side of the lake. It was getting late in the afternoon and, as none of the climbers showed up, we decided to go on to our destination at Camp Douglas. After our arrival, it didn't take us long to establish camp. We had time to take a little warm-up climb. It turned out to be much more than a warm-up.

"About a quarter-of-a-mile away from the camp, there is a sandstone formation called Devil's Monument. It is about 130 feet high, and the only way to the top is by climbing. We decided to climb the southwest ridge. It was climbed once before by Fritz Wiessner, and he recommended it as a good climb.

"It was getting dark before we started, but the climb was not long, and we were soon at the top. We climbed down the west side.

"With the rope around my hips, I started out. Jack belayed me, and I went down approximately 30 to 40 feet. There I found a little ledge from where I could belay the fellows coming down. It was quickly getting dark when Jack, who was second, pulled in beside me. I moved over on the ledge about 15 feet from Jack where I could secure him and, at the same time, watch Paul climb down. I had it in mind to go another ten feet, where there was a little tree. I figured on using it for a rappel.

"First, though, Paul had to come down, so I waited. Jack belayed Paul. I had a 15-foot rope between Jack and me, and I held it tight. Paul must have been about 15 feet above Jack when I heard him yell, 'Watch out!' I had my eyes on him and saw him go off the wall. Like a human bird, he flew out in the air. All I could do was put more tension on the rope between Jack and I, and wait for whatever was going to happen next. A second later, I saw Jack fall backwards off the edge where he had been sitting. I brought him to a quick stop. Then, everything was quiet for a few seconds. I heard Jack calling that he was hit on the head by a rock and had a hole in the back of his head. He was bleeding badly.

"I called for Paul, and he answered. He assured me that he was all right. I couldn't believe him. I thought he was just saying that so we wouldn't get excited. He called from below and told me to take care of Jack. I climbed down to Jack.

"Jack's shirt was drenched with blood. He wanted me to watch him because he still felt a bit dizzy from the hit on his head. I called Paul again. He said that he wouldn't mind having a few feet of rope because he was hanging in the air and wasn't very comfortable. I managed somehow to give him about five feet of rope. He then could get a little hold on a very smooth chimney, close to where he was hanging. After I got a foothold, Paul took over the rope and climbed down the rest of the chimney until he was on the base of the rock. Now I could take care of Jack. With a temporary bandage, we brought the bleeding to a stop. He wasn't sure if he could rappel or climb down without having trouble, so I lowered him down on a rope to Paul.

"Both of them were worried about me getting down. It was completely dark by now. I pulled up a rope and rolled it so I could climb over to the tree, from where I wanted to rappel. Meanwhile, Paul went to the car and turned the lights on over against the rock wall. I found my way easily. I put the center of the rope around the three-inch tree and tossed both ends over the wall. The rope was 120-feet long, so it gave me almost a 60-foot rappel to a little shoulder from where I could climb the rest of the way down without a rope.

"Paul came up to the end of the rope with the flashlight. We continued down the rest of the wall and met Jack. We all shook hands and were very happy that everything came out this well.

"I left the rope up there because it was twisted. It would be easy to get it down the next day.

"Well, one thing is sure. We proved that a good rope and a good belay can save lives.

"We went back to camp, made a fire and, after heating some water, gave Jack first-aid. In addition to the hole in his head, Jack had a 12-inch rope burn over his left arm and shoulder.

"Paul fell 30 feet before the rope stopped him. At that moment, it must have slid over Jack's arm quite a length before Paul came to a complete halt.

"When we had fixed Jack up with bandages as well as we could, we sat by the camp fire and talked about all kinds of climbing experiences we had had. After we tired of singing and talking, we turned in. Jack must have had some night, as he was turning around quite often.

"Morning came, and we were ready for another day's climb. Ragged Towers, about three miles from our camp, was our next objective. Of course, I had to climb up on Devil's Monument to get the rope down. We wanted this rope badly because it had been on the American K-2 Expedition in the Himalayan Mountains[16], and had now saved Paul's (and maybe Jack's) life.

"I took the opportunity of measuring the distance Paul fell. It was 54 feet, and all he got out of it was a little mark on his back from the rope.

"At Ragged Towers, there are four towers that lean on one another. On the third highest, there is some kind of crack which broadens and separates into a chimney. It was not very complicated and we climbed up the crack to the top of the third tower. Then we rested on the top in a notch between the third and fourth towers. From here we could study the last 30 feet up to the highest tower. At first, it was very smooth. Then there was a stretch of about ten feet that was all overhanging. It looked very hard to climb, but not impossible.

"I set up our movie camera.

"Paul took a few pitons and carabiners. While Jack belayed, Paul started up the little crack. He reached as high as he could and drove in a piton. I was sure that this piece of overhang had to be climbed without a stop, and I enjoyed how Paul did it this way.

"After he went over the top, he paused for a while and called down, 'Boy, this was plenty tough.' Paul belayed me from the top, and I didn't find it any easier than he did. We had to leave the piton in the wall because it was in too tight.

"We had two ropes, a 100-foot rope and a 120-foot rope, along for this climb, and they came in handy. We rappeled down the 100-foot wall of the tower, but we needed more than 200 feet of rope. It was quite a slide down.

"This was the end of our climbing trip. We went back to camp, packed up our belongings and left for Chicago.

"Satisfied with the outcome of our trip, we will always remember this little experience of rock climbing."

Joe's prediction about memory turned out to be correct. Fifty-five years later, both Joe and Fralick "remember this little experience" in vivid detail. Joe related the story at considerable length, almost exactly like his 1941 narrative. He questioned whether Jack had been hit by a rock. More likely, Joe thought, he had hit his head on the edge of the ledge when Paul's fall pulled him off.

Fralick's memory is equally as vivid. "It was nearly dark. Joe descended first to a ledge. I followed him down to the ledge where he anchored me. Paul descended last and fell when a handhold broke. He was 15 feet above my belay and fell about 40 feet below me, thus taking about 25 feet of rope from me as it slid over my shoulder and arm. I still have the scar from that rope burn. In the process, I was pulled over the edge of the ledge for about six feet. I believe I stopped Paul's fall. In any case, it is safe to say that Joe's backup belay saved all of us."

Fralick wrote about Paul's climb of the double-overhanging crack in the December 1941 issue of *Appalachia*:

> Paul Stettner elected to climb the Southeast Face [of the highest of the Ragged Towers] despite [the] double overhang in the final wall. I cannot remember or imagine anything more difficult. In fact, I followed Wiessner's route as a second on the rope, while Joe, coming third, was able to overcome the double overhang led

Joe on Longs Peak in 1942.

Bob Ormes on Stettner Ledges in 1942.

Joe climbing on an unidentified wall, probably in the Indian Peaks area in 1942.

by Paul. This is not to say that Wiessner's party could not have negotiated the double overhang. It is to say that he, a master of sandstone, thought better of it.[17] Just the night before this amazing bit of rock climbing, Paul Stettner had fallen 54 feet while descending the Devils Monument in the same area and had been held by the rope.

Seeking out new climbing challenges in the Midwest was not our climbers' only concern. By the end of 1941, the United States had declared war on Japan; Japan and Germany had declared war on the United States; and the U.S. had declared war on Germany. Although wide-spread mobilization loomed heavily, most of 1942 proved to be a year of preparation for war. This, however, did not keep our climbers from the mountains. There was some quiet before the storm.

Joe went to Rocky Mountain National Park with Edith Riedl and Alma Grimmich to do some climbing, and to film climbing sequences for Lee Orr of Magic Carpet of Fox Movietone News. This particular episode was named *The Sensational Sport of Mountaineering*. Joe did some dramatic climbing for the film, sometimes getting as much as three feet off the ground, Joe liked to point out.

During the filming, Joe met Bob Ormes, who was helping Fox Movietone News film the sequences. Ormes, as will be remembered, had claimed to have done the first ascent of the Stettner route on Lone Eagle Peak. He wanted to do the Ledges and asked Joe to climb it with him. And so, fifteen years after the first ascent of the Stettner Ledges, Joe led the third ascent.[18]

By the end of 1942, however, the lives of our mountaineers were indeed affected. Joe volunteered for the army, and Paul, more than a year later, was drafted. Both were assigned to the Tenth Mountain Division.

Fralick was in the Naval Reserve, entered the V-7 program and was commissioned an ensign. He became a "90-day wonder." He entered into service in December of 1942, served in New Guinea for a year-and-a-half, and was discharged in 1945. He then returned to Chicago.

The Plumleys served their country as well, but didn't return to Chicago at the war's end. Bill became an Army Air Corps weather officer and forecaster. He was stationed in the Mariana Islands during the war, where he forcasted upper-air winds over the Japanese islands for the XXI Bomber Command.[19] After discharge, he settled in California. His older brother Harold was stationed in California and elected to remain there. They therefore ended their association with the Chicago Mountaineering Club. Forty-eight years later, during the Club's 50th Anniversary, Bill Plumley was surprised to learn that the club he helped found still existed.

chapter 13

The Tenth Mountain Division

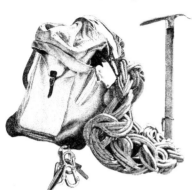

*I*n 1925, when Joe left Germany, he also left politics behind — or so he thought. "I had become," as he put it, "a marked man myself."

America promised a new future, a new culture and new opportunities devoid of Nazis and politics. Yet, excluding politics totally from his life, as his older brother Max had done after his ordeal at the hands of the early Nazis, was a goal not easily achieved. The Nazis "got more and more power," Joe said, and had taken control of all of Germany by the mid-1930s and were occupying Poland, France, the Netherlands and Norway by the early 1940s. Joe could not ignore these realities.

"It was my duty to do something about this," Joe explained many years later. "I knew there was little I could do myself, but I was convinced that I had to do what I could. Hitler and the Nazis had to be stopped. He had hurt me enough. So I decided I had to volunteer for military service."

In the meantime, nearly two years before the Japanese attacked Pearl Harbor, and the United States and Germany exchanged declarations of war, Charles "Minnie" Dole, founder of the National Ski Patrol, and several other crack skiers were discussing the effectiveness and daring of the Finnish ski troops in their lightning attacks on invading Russian forces.[20] The escapades of the Finns in their white camouflage suits, gliding silently on their white skis, had fired the imagination of Dole and his friends.

During this time, Americans were growing increasingly concerned about the possibility of a German attack on the northeast coast of the United States. "What this country needs are mountain troops trained in winter warfare and accustomed to the kind of weather [a blizzard] we are having outside our window tonight," Dole reportedly said to his friends.

In July of 1940, he wrote President Roosevelt to advocate the use of skiers' skills in the military service. Dole suggested that it "is more reasonable to make soldiers out of skiers than skiers out of soldiers." Not discouraged by bureaucratic brush-offs of his ideas, Dole went to Chief of Staff General George C. Marshall and proposed that his National Ski Patrol be used as guerrillas or army scouts because "no group was more familiar with the woods, trails, roads and mountains of the Northeast." General Marshall was impressed.

Soon the Secretary of War set up a pilot program for selected persons to learn ski and snowshoe use and the fundamentals of winter warfare. By the summer of 1941, an advisory committee, formed by the National Ski Association, began experimenting and testing light ski and mountaineering equipment. During the winter of 1940-41, six divisions were selected for winter training in various parts of the country.

In 1941, the Italians invaded the Albanian mountains with dramatic and disastrous consequences — 25,000 killed and 10,000 frozen to death. The lesson was too clear for the American military to ignore. It accepted the necessity for ski-mountaineering troops. In November of 1941, the First Battalion of the 87th Infantry Mountain Regiment was activated at Fort Lewis, Washington. This unit became the nucleus of what was to become the Tenth Mountain Division.

The 87th Infantry was soon expanded to include 4,000 men. A new and larger training site became necessary. Construction of Camp Hale in Colorado was begun in the summer of 1942 at a cost of $28 million.[21] The army selected a small test force to occupy the camp that first winter.

Crest of the Tenth Mountain Division.

Joe learned of the Tenth Mountain Division that summer and sensed immediately that the Tenth would offer him a unique opportunity to make a significant contribution to the American war effort and to bring down Hitler and the Nazis. He volunteered for military service and applied for assignment to the Tenth Mountain Division.

Although inspired by skiers, the military goal was to develop mountain troops. Thus the army sought elite mountaineers, as well as skiers. An emphasis was placed on rock climbing, ice climbing, crampon work and rappelling — all areas that Joe had mastered long ago.

The army also emphasized physical fitness, "toughness," "exceptional stamina," and the ability to "take it," to use Dr. Gretchen Besser's words. To assure that only top, qualified personnel enlisted, the army designated Minnie Dole's National Ski Patrol System (NSPS) and the American Alpine Club to decide on applicant qualifications. These organizations, in turn, required that all applications offer letters of recommendation.

Joe asked Jack Fralick to write his letter of recommendation. By this time, Fralick had learned a great deal about Joe's climbing expertise and recommended him highly. The American Alpine Club also recommended that Joe act as a climbing instructor.

Although already 41 years old, and thus ineligible for overseas service, Joe was exceedingly well qualified in all designated areas — skiing, climbing, toughness and stamina. So the army took him. He became a soldier in October of 1942; the army assigned Private Stettner to Company L, 87th Infantry, Tenth Mountain Division, and stationed him at Fort Carson, and later at Camp Hale, which was nestled in a high valley at 9,500 feet on the western slope of Tennessee Pass in Colorado.

Joe's duty was mountaineering instruction. He was not the only hot climber and skier assigned to Camp Hale. Walter Prager, the Dartmouth and U.S. Ski Team coach, Friedl Pfeiffer, the coach of the American Olympic team, Peter Gabriel, famous Swiss mountaineer, Paul Petzoldt, the outstanding Teton mountaineer and guide and Werner von Trapp of *Sound of Music* fame were also there.

Joe developed warm friendships with Prager and Gabriel, with Pepi Teichner, an Austrian ski instructor, and Dino Sarino, a former officer with the Italian mountain troops. He would treasure these friendships for the rest of his life. He also ran into an old friend, Earl Clark[22], a charter member of the Chicago Mountaineering Club.

Joe remembers a very international group, composed of Germans, Swiss, Austrians, Swedes, Italians and Norwegians, most of whom were immigrants who had learned mountaineering and skiing in Europe. He called them the "International Brigade." They often were

Private Joe Stettner stretches to clip into a piton on a training climb near Camp Hale. (Courtesy Denver Public Library, Western History Collection)

Joe Stettner on skis at Camp Hale during the winter of 1942-43.

extremely anti-fascist and thus shared not only a common love of mountain sports, but also a common political viewpoint, which motivated them and molded them into a "tightly knit fraternity." Joe described them as a "bunch of tough guys."

Age offered Joe little advantage and no breaks. The demands of infantry training at altitude were great. Rank played a lesser role in the Tenth Mountain Division than was typical in the military. Enlisted men often instructed their outranking officers. This was the case with Joe. Although Lt. Peterson was in charge of Company L, Joe — though only a private — became Peterson's second in command.

According to Joe, he became a "special man in the outfit." He was selected to provide climbing instruction to high-ranking officers and gave regular climbing demonstrations to the 87th Infantry. He even developed what was described as a "splendid rock-climbing movie" for instruction purposes.[17]

For a short period, Joe was assigned to the 126th Engineers to instruct them in climbing, and to help determine how to transport heavy military equipment over the mountains. The "hi-tech" engineers learned that mules were of great importance in hauling equipment over mountain passes. So mules became commonplace. The lead mule was named "Minnie," in tribute to founding father Minnie Dole. Even more hi-tech was Joe's idea to develop an ice climbing wall. He encouraged the 126th Engineers to pipe water up a slope and over a cliff. The frozen ice became an ideal place to practice challenging ice-climbing.

Training for the Tenth Mountain Division took place five days a week, regardless of conditions. The weekends, however, were left free, and the soldiers were regularly given passes. The spirit of these weekends was well expressed by the lyrics of a favorite 10th Mountain Division ditty:

At Camp Hale in 1942 with (left to right) Max Eberli, visitor Alma Grimmich, Earl Clark and Joe.

SYSTEMS AND THEORIES OF SKIING

There are systems and theories of skiing,
  But one thing I surely have found,
While skiing's confined to the wintertime,
  The drinking's good all the year round.

Oh — Here's to the trail on the mountain top,
  And here's to the skier who dares!
But give me my glass and my bottle,
  To drive away all of my cares.

There's the snowplow, the stem turn, the christie,
  The jump turn, the telemark and such,
But I leave these all to the kanonon,
  'Cause I like my drinking so much.

Oh — Here's to the trail on the mountain top,
  And here's to the skier who dares!
But give me my glass and my bottle,
  To drive away all of my cares.

Now the skier must dodge all the trees-he-sees,
  And the rocks that lie hidden in the trail,
But the things I fear most are the heebee-jeebees,
  And the Snow-snake's loud, hideous wail.

Oh — Here's to the trail to the mountain top,
  And here's to the skier who dares!
But give me my glass and my bottle,
  To drive away all of my cares.

Soldiers look at the Cross Couloir from Notch Mountain in December of 1943.
(Courtesy Denver Public Library, Western History Collection)

Joe took advantage of none of these bibulous weekends. Rather, he, and three or four of his buddies, would either rope up and go climbing or take their skis into the mountains.

In the winter of 1943, Joe, fellow CMC friend Earl Clark and six other ski-troopers, with the support of the 10th Mountain Division, attempted an ascent of the famous "Cross Couloir" of the Mount of the Holy Cross near Vail. They made it to the top of Notch Mountain and could see the Cross Couloir beaconing to the west, but time and weather prevented a successful ascent.

Joe didn't like the army-issue skis, supplied by Groswald of Denver. They were too stiff and were unsuitable for deep snow. Joe vented his frustrations in letters to Paul, who responded by painting Joe's old skis white, like the general issue ones, and sending them to him at Camp Hale. Though "out of uniform," his own disguised skis converted Joe into a happy Camp Hale camper.

Skis were not the only problem. General-issue ice ax handles broke and crampons fractured. Gradually the Tenth Mountain Division learned from its bad experiences and, slowly but surely, the equipment improved. Eventually the "ski troopers" became well-equipped.[18]

So did the Tenth Mountain Division. As Dr. Besser wrote in her article:

[C]amouflage had to be complete to be effective. Even a tiny speck of black — a pair of sunglasses, a rifle strap — could give away an entire platoon. Everything the men wore and carried was white, including reversible parkas and hoods, their rifles and packs, their skis and the spats that covered their boots. Pete Austin, who was attached to the Tenth, recalls sitting with his battalion commander at dawn one morning, watching an entire battalion — 1,200 men — supposedly moving across the floor of the valley below. "It was uncanny," said Austin. "We knew the men were passing right down there in front of us," he says, "but we couldn't see a thing."

At the completion of this phase of training in the summer of 1943, the 87th Infantry was moved to Fort Ord, California, supposedly to be shipped overseas. Because Joe was over 40, he was not — at his rank — eligible for overseas service.

In the meantime, his civilian company back in Chicago, Liquid Carbonic, had received a large defense contract to produce metal work for airplane engines and exhaust systems. The company desperately needed Joe's highly developed skills as a metal worker to instruct others (mainly women) in the art of metal work and welding. The company wrote to the army and requested that, if the army did not need Joe any longer, he be discharged and returned to Liquid Carbonic:

The Liquid Carbonic Corporation
Chicago
J.H. Pratt
Eexecutive Vice President
April 12, 1943

To Whom It May Concern:

We are desirous of obtaining the services of Pvt. Joseph Stettner as an expert sheet metal worker. He has been employed prior to his induction into the Army by this company for a great many years and at the time he left us was a supervisor in charge of our spot welders.

We have a contract for collector rings and tail pipes for airplane engines from Curtiss-Wright and Republic and we have been informed that our production must be materially increased over the original schedule. A man of Pvt. Stettner's ability and experience will be of great value to us and in our opinion he will be of more value to the war effort as a mechanic than as a soldier. We stand ready to re-employ him at his regular rate of pay just the minute he can be released from the Army.

Yours truly,
J.H. Pratt

This resulted in Joe's honorable discharge in June of 1943. He returned to civilian life, to his soon-to-be wife Edith and to *Wanda Welder* — that is, to the many young women of Liquid Carbonic, eager to learn the art of welding and aid the nation's military effort.

The Tenth Mountain Division remained stateside for a year, eventually being transferred to southwest Texas. The wisdom of not sending the Tenth immediately overseas was questioned. The army claimed this move was necessary to "round out their experience." Whatever the reasoning, the transfer to Texas resulted in ferocious grumbling by both soldiers and mules.

In the meantime, Paul and Anne, who now had a five-year-old son, Paul Jr., sensed that Paul would soon be drafted. He was of a draftable age (37) and not employed by the defense industry. He took the initiative and paid a visit to the draft board to discuss his situation. "If I am drafted," Paul requested, "I want to be assigned to the 10th Mountain Division."

In anticipation of the inevitable, Paul asked his friend, John Ebert, President of the Iowa Mountaineers, to write to the army in support of his request to be assigned to the 10th Mountain Division:

> Iowa Mountaineers
> State University of Iowa
> Iowa City, Iowa
> Founded 1939
> November 2, 1943
>
> To Whom It May Concern:
>
> This is to inform you that I am intimately acquainted with one PAUL STETTNER, of CHICAGO, ILLINOIS. Mr. Stettner is an expert mountain climber and skier and is at home in the outdoors, especially in the primitive and mountainous regions. He has guided large groups of our members on many occasions and has always impressed us with his outstanding ability and clean-cut personality. We have always found him physically and morally above reproach, and a good American citizen in both thought and deed.
>
> Very truly yours,
> Sylvanus J. Ebert
> President, Iowa Mountaineers

On the same day, Paul sent a completed questionnaire to the National Ski Association in his effort to gain assignment to the "Mountain Troops." Paul's sense of the inevitable was accurate, and his and Ebert's efforts were successful. On January 19, 1944, Paul reported for duty at Ft. Sheridan, Illinois, and became a soldier.

Assigned to the 10th Mountain Division, he was stationed at Camp Wolters, Texas, where he learned to "soldier" after intensive infantry training. There was no mountain training there. In June of 1944, he was transferred to dismantle Camp Hale, an effort that took only ten days — then back to Texas, this time to Camp Swift, the major location of the Tenth Mountain Division. In one of many letters to Anne, Paul complained that in Texas, "everything down here either bites or stings you."

The Tenth didn't remain in Texas forever. Things began to change in November of 1944, when the Army assigned Major General George P. Hays to command the Tenth Mountain Division. General Hays was a fighter. He had won a Medal of Honor, two Silver Stars, the Croix de Guerre with Palm, the Legion of Honor and the Purple Heart. He also had spent 163 consecutive days on the front lines after having landed in France on D-Day plus one.

A month after taking over command, General Hays took the first ship load of Tenth Mountain troops to Naples, Italy. Paul and his 87th Infantry, Joe's old regiment, were part of this group. The 87th Infantry Regiment set sail on January 3, 1945. They found the situation on arrival in Italy to be normal — namely, all fouled up. There were no sleeping bags, mules or other mountain gear that the troops had been trained to use. Apparently, at some high level, a general officer had concluded this equipment would not be necessary and left it at home. This naturally caused a delay.

But on February 15, 1945, the Tenth Mountain Division received a field order:[23]

> 10th Mountain Division will attack on D-Day to seize, occupy, organize, and defend the Mt. Belvedere-Mt. della Torraccia ridge, prepare for action to the northeast.

The challenge was great. As Dr. Besser wrote:

> The job facing the Tenth Mountain Division was nothing less than breaking through the German Gothic line, which followed the crest of the Apennines some 35 miles north of Florence. German forces had controlled these high peaks and ridges for months, and it seemed nothing could dislodge them. Three times the Fifth Army had attempted to assault Mt. Belvedere, the loftiest point between the Allied Forces and the Po Valley, and three times it had been repelled. Now it was the Tenth's turn to make the try, its first combat mission.

*Paul Stettner in 1943,
before going overseas.*

Mt. Belvedere had a steep cliff on one side and a gentle slope on the other. The German forces were concentrated on the gentle side; and they considered the cliff side impregnable. The Tenth Mountain Division conceived a daring plan — surprise the Germans by climbing the vertical face. Dr. Besser describes the attack:

> Reconnaissance parties were sent out to chart crude routes up the rocky wall. Under cover of darkness on the night of February 18, 1945, 800 expert rock climbers, heavily laden with rifles, ammunition and 89mm mortars, began to pick their way stealthily up the icy, almost perpendicular cliff. At every moment, they expected a rain of bullets from above. Astonishingly, they made the climb undetected. As they scrambled over the top at daybreak, they had no trouble in overcoming the astounded German holding force, who had never anticipated an assault from that quarter.
>
> Once the German positions were captured, the Tenth had to fight off wave after wave of counterattacks. The battles for Belvedere, Riva Ridge, and nearby Monte della Toraccia were brutal and bitter. At the end of two weeks of remorseless combat, the Tenth Mountain Division had sustained more than 850 casualties.

After this remarkable victory, the Tenth Mountain Division engaged in bloody skirmish after bloody skirmish, as it worked its way northward over mountain ranges and through mountain valleys. They fought mostly at night.

Paul played an important role in the capture of Mt. Belvidere. During the second day (March 4, 1945) of the second offensive, Paul's unit, the First Platoon of Company F, attempted to establish outposts on a ridge running out of Natale and moved to take control of Gualandi on the regimental left boundary. As the patrol approached Gualandi, according to historian George Earle:

> They were fired on by snipers. The men all took cover, all except Private First Class Paul Stettner, who braved the fire to continue moving forward shouting in German to surrender for they were out numbered. This action drew fire, confused the enemy and allowed the remainder of the patrol to enter the town and capture thirteen Germans.

For his bravery, Paul received the Silver Star. The citation read:

Headquarters
10TH Mountain Division
APO #345
U.S. Army
27 March 1945

CITATION

PAUL, STETTNER, 36783170, Private First Class, Infantry, United States Army. For gallantry in action on 4 March 1945, near Gualandi, Italy. When accurate sniper fire was directed at the patrol approaching to clear a village of the enemy, the patrol's advance was halted and its members compelled to seek cover. Private First Class STETTNER, one of the men in the patrol, unmindful of his comrades seeking cover and heedless of the hazardous fire, continued to make his way forward while shouting to the enemy in their own language to surrender and that they were outnumbered. This daring action attracted the enemy fire and so startled them that the remainder of the patrol was able to enter the town and capture eighteen of the enemy. Such determination and gallant courage displayed in this action enabled the accomplishment of an important mission with no casualties. The bravery and high regard for duty of Private First Class STETTNER inspired all who observed them and are deserving of much praise.

Entered the military service from Chicago, Illinois.

By command of Major General Hays:

H.F. Miller
Major, AGD
Asst. Adj. Gen.

According to historian George Earle:

> During this three day battle, the 87th lost in total battle casualties 155 men . . . It cleared the enemy from a mountainous area over 6,000 yards deep into his territory, and 2,000 to 3,000 yards wide. Six hundred German soldiers and officers were captured and driven through the PW cage during the three day period. An unknown number of enemy dead and quantities of enemy armament and equipment were removed from the occupied mountains.

On April 14, 1945, the Tenth began a second campaign to capture the Po Valley. Their aggressiveness brought them 40 miles beyond their own supply lines. Without much intelligence, aerial photographs or air support, they made a daring river crossing at night and under heavy artillery fire, and secured the enemy side of the Po Valley. They soon liberated Verona and continued their pursuit of German troops that fled toward the Brenner Pass. The German Army attempted to blockade the mountain tunnels to stop the Tenth's advance. But one battalion inched its way up a rock cliff to take the enemy from above, a brilliant maneuver that practically brought an end to German resistance in the south. On May 2, 1945, church bells pealed to signal the German surrender.

At the war's end, the Tenth Mountain Division received great praise. General Mark Clark called the Tenth Mountain Division "the finest Division I have ever seen" and its action "one of the most vital and brilliant in the Italian campaign."[24] Upon surrendering in Italy, German General von Senger of the 14th Panzer Corps declared the Tenth to be the best division he had faced on the Russian, Sicilian or Italian fronts.

Perhaps the most important sentiment was expressed by the Tenth Mountain Division's own commander, General George Hays:

> Because of your special training in mountain warfare, you were assigned the most important and hazardous mission of any division in the Italian theater. You were directed to spearhead the Fifth Army in its final attack on the German Armies . . . There have been more heroic deeds crammed into these days than I ever heard of . . .

Paul remained with the Tenth Mountain Division, which moved northward to Salzburg, Austria. Salzburg is about 70 miles from Munich, Paul's birthplace and his family's residence. He sought permission to visit Munich to see if any of his family were still alive. In an extraordinary move, the army gave Paul, who had been promoted to Staff Sergeant, the following authorization:

Headquarters Company
United States Forces in Austria
AP0 777, U.S. Army
18 August 1945

     This is to authorize S/Sgt. Paul Stettner, 3683170, Hq. & Hq. Co, United States Forces in Austria to be absent from his organization and visit relatives in Munich, Germany from 18 August to 21 August 1945.

For the Commanding Officer:

Daniel R. Baker
1st Lt, Infantry

     To his great joy, Paul found his mother and his youngest sister still living in their family home, which had been seriously damaged during an Allied bombing attack. Apparently, the three-story house had been hit, but the Stettners escaped to the basement. The top floors were destroyed, and they had to be dug out of the basement.

     Paul then found his two older sisters and their families, as well as his oldest brother Max and his family. By the greatest fortune, they all had escaped injury.

     Paul once remarked that neighbors were totally astounded to see him, decked out in his American soldier's uniform, going *spazieren* (strolling) through his old neighborhood with his mother on one arm and his youngest sister on the other.

     Paul was given a second authorization to visit his family, but orders were issued directing him to return home. He was shipped back to the States and discharged in October of 1945.

     Once again he was with Anne, young Paul Jr., Joe, Edith and the Chicago Mountaineering Club.

     It is a reflection of Paul's personality that he never mentioned his acts of valor or his Silver Star to Anne. Several years later, he was awarded a "meritorious service award" by Illinois Governor Dwight Green. Upon inquiry about the meaning of this, Anne learned that her husband was a war hero.[25] Paul must have thought that this aspect of his life was no more noteworthy than the climbs of Stettner Ledges, Lone Eagle Peak and the many other mountaineering feats the Stettners felt to be unworthy of mention. "It vas no big thing," Paul once muttered when asked about his acts of valor.

chapter **14**

Joe and I were sipping some of his eggshell-style coffee and discussing sport climbers one icy November morning. We were noting how these young "rock jocks" are doing climbs that make Stettner Ledges look intermediate. Joe worked hard on this theme, but it became increasingly obvious that his mind and heart were not on climbing. He soon abandoned his efforts to his real concern — his loss of Edith.[26]

"Edith was such a smart cookie," Joe said. I could feel his sense of pride emerging through his obvious grief. "She worked for the Brach Candy Company as a chemist; she did research in candy making. Later she taught chemistry at Schurz High School on Milwaukee Avenue. Edith went to the University of Chicago and was proficient in four languages. Hungarian, of course, was her native language, but she also spoke German, English and Spanish. She studied Russian too.

"She was really smarter than me," Joe said. "I was lucky to find her. I was more lucky that she wanted to be with me. I appreciated her so much as a human being. She had so much talent. Do you know, Jack, I've got to get over this. Here we are talking about climbing, and all I'm doing is thinking about Edith.

"I met her at a Chicago Mountaineering Club outing. She was with the Prairie Club. Some of its members, Edith Riedl, Georgina Fitzgerald and Groves Kilbourn, joined up with the Chicago Mountaineering Club on one of its outings.

"Edith and I had climbed together a little, but one time I drove

Edith at Devils Lake.

her home from Devils Lake. We sat in my car and talked and talked until late. Edith invited me to her place to have some coffee and to meet her mother. I was hesitant to do this, but did so anyway. I didn't think I was good enough or educated enough for Edith.

"One evening she kissed me and hugged me. My heart burst. I was in my forties and had had so many experiences in life and had done so much. But when Edith kissed me, I wanted to put all this behind me.

"It was like crossing over a ridge. Now I was on the other side. And I knew what I wanted.

"Before that kiss, Paul was probably the closest person in the world to me." Joe stared off into space for a minute and then crossed two fingers. "But then Edith came into my life.

"In 1942, Edith, Alma Grimmich, who later married Max Eberli, and I went to Colorado. We stayed a couple of nights with my old friend Charley Hewes at the Kirkwood Inn."

It might be of interest at this point to read some of Joe's notes about this trip, written shortly after his return:

"It was in July, 1942 that I decided to take another trip to the Colorado mountains. For company I asked Edith Riedl and Alma Grimmich of the CMC to come along. I knew the girls, their ability in climbing, and their spirit. I climbed enough with them before. I promised to take them up Longs Peak by way of the Alexanders Chimney. I knew the route, as I climbed it several times before, and I knew that they could do it quite well. I suggested we camp together, and

Joe on Alexanders Chimney, 1942

use my two man tent that was large enough for three . . ."

This was strictly a m o u n t a i n e e r i n g judgment, it appears. Many years later, Jack Fralick observed that "before the War, no romance was apparent."

"Later Edith and I climbed Alexanders Chimney on Longs Peak, just like Paul and Anne did many years before. We also climbed the Arapahos and Navajo and Apache. Edith was a strong hiker.

"But then the war came. I volunteered and was assigned to the Tenth Mountain Division in Colorado. I remember leaving Chicago. It's so clear in my mind. I left Union Station. It was 1942. Edith and Paul and several friends went with me to the station to say good-bye and wish me a good farewell.

"Edith and I went off to park the car, which gave us a few minutes alone. I said, 'If I don't come back, you can have everything.' She replied, 'And if you do come back, I'll be here.'" As Joe related this story, his emotions welled up and he cried. "It wasn't long before I was having Thanksgiving dinner at Fort Carson.

"Edith and I wrote a lot of letters to each other. During this time, Edith went skiing with Paul and broke her right arm. I know it was a lot of trouble for her to write letters to me with her left hand, and I was touched by her effort; but the truth is, these letters were a lot easier to read.

"When I returned from Camp Hale, I came to Edith. 'I'm back,' I said. 'Where do you think we should live?'

"'My mother and sister are getting another apartment,' Edith answered. 'We can live in our place.'

"As I think back about this, it all seems to have been well calculated. But I wasn't thinking that at the time because then she really kissed me. And nothing else mattered. I was a teenager again. My heart jumped out. This was it. She accepted my proposal. I was the happiest man in the world. It was the happiest time of my life.

"Do you know, Jack, if you are honest with yourself, you know when the time comes. With my first marriage, I had a sense that it wasn't the right time or the right way. Then I got divorced and wasn't married for ten years. I could do anything. I saw a lot of people, and I learned a lot.

"So when Edith kissed me I knew it was not a false thing. I knew it was right.

"When I took Edith home from Devils Lake outings, I was never pushy or fresh. I held back. I always thought, 'If you want a woman, you should live with her.' I felt this way about all women, not just Edith.

"A long time ago in Germany when I was a young man, I was seeing a young woman quite a bit. I've told you about her. It was Hanni Arnold, the girl I climbed the Dreitorspitze with. There had been a couple of good kisses. Nothing more. Nothing serious. But she liked me, and I liked her. One day her parents left, leaving us alone. She was in her bedroom, and I was in the living room. She called me. She said, 'Pepi[27], could you help me button my bra?' I went into her room, buttoned her bra and left. Nothing happened!

"If I was like the kids of today, something would have happened. But I was a mountain climber, and my thoughts and energies went out for sports. And, as I said, if you want to be with a woman, you should live with her. Interestingly, this incident helped develop a lot of trust between us. I was 24 or 25 when I left Germany, but we remained friends for as long as she lived.

"And so I didn't touch Edith before we were married.

"Edith and I got married at City Hall in Chicago. We went to the sand dunes in Indiana for our honeymoon. As we took off, I remembered that I had no bathing suit, so we stopped at a State Street store to get one and then headed for the dunes. We stayed at an old roadhouse. I remember a wonderful card Edith gave me with a little poem she wrote. I still have it. It said:

To my sweet

Since you gave up the other misses,
I am yours with hugs and kisses,
Truly, I am your loving wife,
Hang on your neck, rest of your life.

Edith, 1944

"When we returned home, I first carried a case of beer into our new home, then I carried Edith. The order made sense because after I took Edith up, I knew I wouldn't want to go back.

"We then took a second honeymoon. In spring, we went up to a cabin near Berthoud Pass in Colorado. It was the same cabin Paul and I stayed in in 1940. It had broken windows and was cold. We had a hard time, even though I fixed the windows and tried to get it warmed up. We skied at Winter Park, but the snow was bad. It was icy and frozen.

"Later Edith and I went to the Tetons and, after climbing and hiking, we stopped by a lake to freshen up. I have a wonderful photo of Edith, with forests and the Tetons in the background. It captures the spirit of the moment, and the beauty of nature, and Edith and the towering mountains.

"I wanted to make Edith happy, and she was. I think she was happy from the first moment we married.

"I really didn't want a family. But Edith was so happy when Ginni came. And this made me very happy, too. It made me happy to see Edith so happy. It would have been OK to have another child, but not three or four. But no more children came.

"Edith was never a jealous person. She was never jealous when I kissed other girls. After the war in 1946, Edith and I went to Germany. I had learned that Hanni had a small grocery store near Rosenheim, so I went there to find her.

"I went into the store and saw Hanni working. I said very critically, 'Is there no service here?' Hanni recognized me immediately. 'Pepi,' she cried. It was wonderful seeing her. She had been married, but her husband had died from sickness during the war. She had a daughter, Helga.

"Later Hanni and her brother Rudi came to America to visit Paul. Paul and Rudi had been classmates. Rudi lost his wife during the bombing of Germany, but now had a new wife.

"We all got together — Hanni and Rudi, Paul and Anne, Edith and I. We had a great time. Edith's mother was very suspicious of Hanni and let us know of her suspicions. But Edith was not jealous and became a great friend of Hanni.

"Hanni was a nice woman. But I wouldn't have changed anyone for Edith. I wouldn't have been as happy with Hanni. Now both are gone.

"One time I made a ladle for Edith. You've seen it. It is simple, modern looking. I never thought it was worth too much, but Edith loved it and valued it. And this caused the ladle to have great importance to me. Edith's love did this.

"Edith was very forgiving. This helped and taught me a lot. One time when we were climbing, we packed wood up to a hut where we planned to stay. Lothar Kolbig, who was one of our group, decided to go down, and took the wood with him. This upset and hurt me a lot. It made me angry. Climbers simply don't do that.

"But Edith said, 'Lothar is all right. He's a nice fellow.'

"I told Edith that most things don't hit me so hard, but this did. She said, 'Oh, that's alright. I understand how people feel.' That was typical of Edith. She was so nice and understanding, and sweet and forgiving.

"Edith had so many interests. She was interested in the plight of the American Indians. She supported them financially. She supported the Indians in Oklahoma and the Ogalalla Indians. She believed they needed her help. She also supported Alzheimer and cancer research.

"She loved art and the Art Institute of Chicago and often took Ginni there. That's were Ginni got her interest in art. This was one of the reasons why Edith didn't want to leave Chicago.

"But we took many trips. We went to Europe, to Spain, to Alaska and visited and climbed. I drove a bus to Alaska for the Iowa Mountaineers, and Edith came along.

"It was a happy, happy life with Edith. Right now, I realize it more and more. The 50 years I spent with her are not coming back, and so I must be satisfied with what I've had. There'll be no more.

"I've had everything. But life goes on. You've got to enjoy it when you can. When you're dead, you're dead. You can't take anything along.

"I just hope that you find a good woman who loves you, and who you can love.[28] Like I did with Edith." When the old mountaineer said this, he broke down and cried.

After regaining his composure, he said: "Do you know, Jack, the most enjoyable sport is climbing in the mountains. I did everything that I liked. It all came easy. But the most important thing to me was my life with Edith. That made living worthwhile.

"Edith always meant well. She did so much for everybody. Life is just a dream. But with Edith, it was a sweet dream, a dream not wasted, a good dream."

chapter 15

Guiding and Leading

The war had ended and most of the young men came home, hoping to re-establish, as best they could, the life they had left behind. For some young men in Iowa City, home of the Iowa Mountaineers, normal life included climbing. The Iowa Mountaineers started as a University of Iowa climbing club, but over time it had become a commercial venture for its leader John Ebert. Joe and Paul met Ebert before the war. He encouraged them to act as guides and climbing leaders. And so the Stettner brothers began sharing their love of the mountains and climbing expertise with the Iowa Mountaineers.

In 1945, Joe acted as chief guide for the Mountaineers' outing in the Tetons, where he led climbs of all three Tetons, and put up a new route on the South Face of Nez Perce's East Summit with John Speck.

In 1948, Joe again acted as chief guide for the Iowa Mountaineers on their outing to the Wind River Range in Wyoming. During the trip, Ebert planned to stop at Devils Tower in Wyoming and to attempt the Durrance Crack on the East Face of the Tower. According to Joe, Ebert wanted to get ten of his Iowa Mountaineers on the top and bivouac there. To that end, he hired well-known Teton guide and great route finder Paul Petzoldt at a fee of $400 to lead the climb.

Joe remarked that neither he nor his brother Paul had ever employed a guide, and had never taken any money for guiding. You climb for yourself, not for money, Joe believed. The Iowa Mountaineers did, however, pay for Joe and Pauls' expenses on their several Iowa

Mountaineers' trips. They got a free mountaineering trip in exchange for their guiding and leadership.

Late that night, before the attempt on Devils Tower, the Mountaineers were gathered at a camp fire telling tales and singing songs. Petzoldt was there. Joe was not. Ebert halted the festivities to announce the plans for the climb. He named a group and stated that Paul Petzoldt would lead the climb.

Later that night, at about midnight, Joe arrived from the Tetons. Most of the others were asleep by this time. Ebert told him that Petzoldt was going to lead the Durrance Crack, and that Joe would be a second. Joe was silent.

A few minutes later, Joe told Ebert, "Either Paul [Stettner] or I have led every climb I have ever been on.[29] If I don't lead, I don't climb!"

Petzoldt, who was standing nearby, overheard this conversation and interjected, "If Joe wants to do it, let him. I'll belay. It's always good to let a younger man take the lead."

Many years later when Joe related this story, he reported that when Petzoldt referred to him as a "younger man," he thought, "Hold on a second. I'm 10 to 15 years older than Petzoldt."[30] Joe went on to say that Paul Petzoldt was "a big guy and kind of clumsy. He had tried the route before and failed.[31] I think Petzoldt was more than happy to give me the lead," Joe said with a smile.

Joe led and completed the eighth ascent of Devils Tower. Once asked about the Stettners in 1994, Paul Petzoldt reportedly said, "Oh, yes, they were human flies." In his recent book *Teton Tales*, Petzoldt wrote:

> My wife was living with me then, and we were meeting some interesting people who were coming through Jenny Lake, some who stayed quite a while. The Stagners [sic] started showing up. They were some of the first acrobatic climbers I knew. They weren't particularly interested in climbing mountains; they were interested in climbing hard chimneys or cracks. The Stagners were from the Chicago Mountaineering Club and had been circus performers, maybe tightrope walkers or the men of the flying trapeze,[32] but were the first sport climbers I knew. They were impressive, and I learned some techniques from watching them. But these were mostly techniques we didn't need to use on our climbs.

Joe once remarked that he felt more comfortable leading because, as he put it, "I know what I can do."

chapter 16 East Face of Monitor Peak

The war, and all the disruption it inflicted on the lives of CMC members, finally came to an end. The Club's soldiers and sailors, one by one, returned home and attempted to resume a normal life. An important step in that direction was to reactivate the Chicago Mountaineering Club. Not everyone returned to the Chicago area. Amongst the missing were the Plumley brothers. Both Bill and Harold found new professional opportunities in California and Washington, D.C., and left the Chicago area forever.[33]

Fralick and others jump-started the Club by planning two ambitious "Western Outings." The first took place in the Wind River Range in Wyoming in 1946, and the second in the Needle Mountains of the San Juan Range in southwestern Colorado the next summer. The San Juans are the site of several "Fourteeners" (14,000-foot peaks, as they are known in Colorado) and a number of exciting "Thirteeners," including Jagged Mountain, which reminds one of a witch's mountain in a Disney cartoon, and Monitor Peak. The San Juans were a most challenging place for the Club to continue its post-war rebirth.

Before the war in 1937, Dr. H.L. McClintock, of the American Alpine Club and the Colorado Mountain Club, wrote about the East Face of Monitor in *Trail and Timberline*, the Colorado Mountain Club's publication:

> For those who want to try a climb of the first order . . .
> there is the east face of Monitor Peak rising almost vertically for
> more than a thousand feet, but with cracks and chimneys which
> may afford the expert a route to the summit.

Ever the student of mountaineering literature, Fralick found McClintock's article. It attracted Fralick's attention and apparently inspired him, perhaps to the extent of playing a role in the Club's selection of the San Juans in the first place. Earlier in 1947, he had extracted a promise from Joe Stettner to "take him along on a good trip, a rather stiff climb," to use Joe's words. Fralick did not tell Joe what he had in mind. As they say, "It's all in the timing" — best wait for the opportune moment.

The Club had set up its camp at Noname Creek at about 10,700-feet in elevation, a convenient location for all kinds of climbing adventures. After several days of climbing, Fralick sensed that the timing was right. The opportune moment had arrived. As Joe remembers:

"I decided to fulfill my promise to Jack about going on a good trip; a rather stiff climb. While at the campfire, I asked him if he had in mind any particular mountain to climb. Jack mentioned Monitor. A bit to my surprise, he knew all about the mountain. He said that the south side had been climbed several times and was fairly easy. But the southeast ridge and the East Face were unclimbed. His preference was for the East Face. This suited me just fine, for earlier during the outing, I had looked up several times to the 1,200 foot wall of Monitor, and I hoped that one day I would have a chance to try it.

"I knew Jack and his ability well. But I felt that another man would make our party stronger. Three in a climbing group is always safer than two, although much slower. For the third man I asked John Speck. He was an excellent climber, and at this time he was in good condition after three weeks of climbing in the Canadian Rockies. He was willing, and so we decided to leave camp around seven the next morning.

"Our equipment consisted of 120 feet of 7/16th-inch nylon rope, 30 feet of sling rope, 12 pitons, six carabiners, two climbing hammers and sneakers. Actually we had a variety of footwear. Jack had Swiss edging nails, John had rubber-cleat, army ski boots, and I had hard-toe, rubber-soled army shoes. Earlier I had inserted ten steel spikes in each sole, around the edge, that projected 1/8th of an inch from the rubber sole. This gave me a chance to use the rubber on dry rock, while the nails were helpful on wet surfaces."

By following numerous sheep trails, Joe, John and Jack worked their way through the gnarled timber into a lush green meadow, sprinkled with mountain flowers of red, orange, purple and blue. Sheep nibbled

Equipment used on the climb of the East face of Monitor.

enthusiastically on sweet grass. Butterflies added to the erratic pattern of color. Fralick has vivid memories of their approach.

He wrote, "Hiking through beautifully flowered meadows, we finally reached the talus slopes under the eastern base of Monitor. As we drew closer to the mountain, we stopped frequently to examine our objective. The East Fact is unusually impressive and forbidding. Its principal feature is an immense rock wall contained between two very steep gullies. This great central face is fully 1,200 feet high, remarkably smooth and extremely steep. I believe its average angle exceeds 85 degrees. It appeared simply unclimbable to us."

According to Joe, "As we came up on the trail above the timberline, we sighted the East Face. Pausing several times before we got close to the wall, we studied the possibilities for climbs. Somewhat to the south of the main summit there was a gully or what might be called a wide chimney, that led from right to left across the face toward the south ridge. The width of this chimney varied from ten to 30 feet. Its back wall and sides were rather smooth. As we studied the route with binoculars, some of the spots looked very difficult, especially halfway up, where there was a big overhang blocking the way." Not easily discouraged, Joe thought, "We should leave the solution to this obstacle open till we reach it.

"When we got to the base of the wall, we stripped ourselves of

*The East Face of Monitor Peak. Joe's 1947 route
is shown on the left. The route on the right is
that of the second ascent done by Joe's nephew
Paul Jr. with Larry Dalke in 1968. The two
routes joined at about 300 feet from the top.
(Courtesy Colorado Mountain Club)*

everything we could spare, and left it there. It was nine o'clock when we started climbing. The first fifty feet up the gully were easy. After that we stood in front of the vertical wall. I felt that it was too soon to have to rope up.

"I tied into the rope and asked Jack to belay me on the first lead out of the gully. I went to the left, out onto the open face of the mountain. It was not difficult, but after a 30-foot traverse, I felt unsafe and placed the first piton and fastened my rope to the piton with a carabiner." Joe was afraid that if he slipped here he would fall far below his belayer. By placing the piton, he hoped that any fall would "only be double the distance I was above the piton, that is, assuming the belayer was alert and the piton held.

"After this traverse pitch, it got easier. From a good position, I was able to belay Jack and John to my level. The next 50 feet were gained by climbing over a rather open face to the right, toward the gully. We regained the gully above the place we had left it. But soon we were forced back to the left to a three foot crack that led to an overhanging block. By wedging ourselves into the crack, we worked ourselves gradually up and sat down together for a short rest beneath the overhang.

"Then I led out again to the right over the smooth face. I tried to go back to the big gully but was forced back by an impassable smooth wall. However, on the edge of the gully there was a thin plate of rock that made it possible to get three feet higher. By going back toward my partners and well above them, I was able to cut out the direct climb of the overhang. From here there was a long stretch that was very much exposed. At a number of places, we had to climb on slabs that overhung the slabs immediately below. Consequently, at times we saw only thin air and the boulderfield below us."

Fralick recollects this spot. "At least twice we were forced to leave it for a short stretch, always by a traverse to the right. One such traverse was unforgettable. It was made possible only by the existence of certain slight irregularities in the surface of a steeply inclined slab. It required a ticklish bit of climbing on rock as exposed as any likely to be found. The slab overhung the wall below, and the view straight down was uninterrupted for hundreds of feet."

Joe's story continues, "The crack continued to our left. On several occasions we used it for short stretches. Finally it ran into the big gully, so we were able to get back on the original route as we had planned. Belayed by Jack, I started up the steep back wall. This was the only possible route in the U-shaped gully. I was climbing without a pack. Jack and John carried their packs most of the time.

"I was about 30 feet above my partners and standing on a narrow

*Jack Fralick following on
the Monitor Peak climb.*

ledge. Jack followed me. He had some difficulty and stopped about 15 feet below me on another narrow ledge. There was not enough space for both of us on my ledge, so it seemed like a good place to stop. Jack now belayed John as he climbed up with his knapsack on his back. He had some trouble on one spot on the overhanging wall to the right of and below Jack. All the time I was belaying Jack and watching John's progress. John gave the overhang one more try, but one of his handholds gave out and he swung from his position below Jack. This sudden side pull made Jack lose his balance. He went over in a somersault. I brought him to a stop a short distance below where he took off. The boys had only a few light scratches, and so the incident did not upset us in the least."

Fralick's memory is equally vivid. "It was here that John and I thought the climb might be about to end. Tiny fingerholds gave way under John's hands, and he fell. Since he was off to my right and below me, he swung and fell at the same time. In trying to stop his fall I was unable to keep my stance. Instinctively I checked and stopped his rope, too rapidly perhaps, and was pulled off and down to the next ledge about five feet below, doing a somersault en route. Our combined fall came heavily on Joe. But he held both of us on the piton and carabiner through which he was anchoring me. John and I landed in such positions that we could quickly take our weight off the rope. Joe's caution in anchoring me while I belayed John had reaped a handsome reward, for it was only his anchor that prevented this from being more than a bad moment quickly forgotten."

Joe continued, "One more rope length and we were underneath the big overhang, the one that we had seen from the base of the mountain and which, at the time, we did not know how to get around. This overhanging wall was smooth and about 30 feet in height. It was impossible to go straight over it, but we had good equipment. With proper technique, we were not licked yet.

"We had all sorts of ideas as we talked over the situation. To the left along the side wall of the gully there was a thin crack, but it was too thin to get finger holds in it. There was a good chance to drive pitons for a tension and rope-sling climb. On the right side of the wall there was a 30 foot crack approximately three inches wide. The first eight feet of this was practically vertical, but the stretch above it fell back to about sixty degrees, a good opportunity for a lie-back climb. This seemed the better deal of the two. However, in order to get to this crack, we had to cross the gully, which was a very delicate operation as hand and foot holds were scarce. A fall at this point would have meant a swing below the belayer and probably against the other wall. To minimize the danger, I climbed above our location, drove a piton in the thin crack and snapped my carabiner with the rope in it. Then I retreated and started to traverse the gully while John belayed me.

"Jack and John watched me closely, since they had to follow me. Soon I arrived on the other side 20 to 25 feet from them. I drove two pitons in the wall above the narrow ledge where I was standing, one for a belay for myself and one for a rope sling. I hoped to stand in the sling and get a step up on the straight and smooth wall so I could reach the lie-back crack. I made two or three attempts without result. As I was trying to gather my strength for the next try, a big fly flew up ahead of me on this tough spot as if to show me how it should be done.

"I looked down the long overhanging gully, but I did not like the looks of the landing spot. Finally, I decided not to waste more of my energy. A shoulder stand would be easier and would leave me in better condition to do the rather difficult lie-back part above. Up to this time, Jack was the second man and John, the third. I changed the order. Since John was the more experienced climber and 20 pounds lighter, we considered it safer to have him on hand in case Jack needed support. As far as I knew, this climb was above Jack's ability and only by taking the greatest care could we make a successful ascent. So from this point on John followed me.

"He climbed up to the first piton, snapped the rope behind him, which led to Jack. Thus belayed from two sides, he made the traverse to my position. Then John faced the wall, and I went up on his shoulder and from there started up the lie-back crack. All I had on my mind was that there is only one way. And that is up. A retreat here would have been almost impossible without a fall. I puffed and puffed. We were all under great tension. Not a word was said. I couldn't. They didn't. John belayed me. Jack belayed John. We all hoped I could make it. Finally, I reached the spot where the lie-back crack changed to an easy crack swinging to the right. I rolled over flat on my stomach and breathed deeply for some time.

"'That was a lulu!,' I yelled to my friends after I regained my breath. This was one of those stretches where I had little energy left. But I had to make it, so I had to throw in some willpower for good measure. Now John followed me. I had a good belay on him from above, and he was safe. But he had as hard a time with that stretch as I had. He was quite exhausted when he reached me.

"John needed so much rope to climb to me that Jack had to untie. He was approximately 80 feet below us and got pretty stiff sitting around while John and I were climbing. Once John was secure, my next job was to take the rope and throw it down to Jack so I could haul up the packs. I had a number of throws before reaching my object. Recoiling the rope every time I missed seemed endless. Finally I got it right. Together with John, we pulled up the packs. And I repeated the lasso act.

"Jack tied in and climbed up to the piton above him in the same manner that John did. But since he was the last person to climb this part, he placed a double rope through the carabiner and lowered himself so he could traverse. Then he pulled the rope out and left the piton with the carabiner behind. This was the first carabiner we lost, but by this time we had donated a number of pitons to this old mountain. Jack found the crossing difficult, and he suggested that he swing across on the belay rope. He did so, but the nylon rope was very elastic and he landed several feet below the expected point. For a moment he looked very surprised, thinking, perhaps, that we had forgotten to hold him. Then he worked his way up to the rope sling. We gave him moral and physical support, and he went through the qualification test of a stiff climb. Everything went well. In time Jack reached us plenty tired, but cheerful."

Fralick noted that, "Using the rope sling and John's shoulder as footholds, Joe managed to get started in the crack. With hands gripping the right edge and using his feet against the left edge, Joe Stettner did a lie-back up the 30-foot crack and climbed into the steep rocks above it before he could pause for even the briefest respite from his exhausting efforts. It was the hardest work to that point, and it pushed Joe to the limit of his exceptional strength and ability.

"The two other members of the party were obliged to accept some assistance from the rope in the lower part of the lie-back crack. An additional aid which the writer found necessary will be disclosed shortly. First I had to cross the gully. After dropping down on the doubled rope, I attempted to cross the slab. For the first and only time during the climb, I felt that my boot nails were inadequate. Sneakers would have proved helpful at this point, but mine were in one of the rucksacks. And these had been pulled up already. A slip here would have meant a drop and a long swing over against the right wall of the gully, since my companions were well above me and a considerable distance off to the right.

"However, I saw that it was possible to climb a few feet farther down the left side of the gully, which would reduce the arc of any swing over to the right side. Here, the crossing proved no easier, and, in the end, I simply swung across on the rope. The swing was about fifteen feet across, and, due to the elasticity of the nylon rope, I also dropped about ten feet. This was not an altogether pleasant experience. But it got me to the right side of the gully at a point from which it was possible to climb up to the lie-back crack. To negotiate the lower half of the crack, I required the assistance of a rope sling tied to the other end of the climbing rope. Thus, a brilliant piece of leading, augmented by the use of pitons, rope slings, a shoulder stand, and a swing on the rope, enabled our three man party to stand together on the same ledge once again — now looking down upon, rather than up to, the major overhang. Having overcome what we thought would be our greatest difficulty, we were now committed to finishing the climb in the central face."

Returning to Joe's story, "Up to this point I had not looked at my watch or had thoughts of eating, but the valley's long shadows gave me the idea that it was late in the afternoon. No one talked about stopping. Of course, we took rests in between climbs since only one climber moved at a time. Jack and John were very good company for this climb. I could have had better climbers with me, but could not have had better companions. They trusted my leadership and were always cheerful and encouraging, even though they accused me of taking the foot and hand holds along with me. I always told them, 'Nothing to it. It's simple.' I still believed that we would finish the wall the same day. But it was tough going all the way, and I would not have liked to watch someone else lead. I know from previous experience that it is much more exciting to keep an eye on the leader than to do the actual job.

"We went approximately two more rope lengths. On the second part, as I was belaying Jack as the last man, he had some trouble. I admit that the place was exposed but not as difficult by far as the lie-back crack we had just finished. His head appeared above the edge, but he must have slipped a little for he disappeared rather rapidly. He could not have gone more than a few feet, as the rope yielded only a little. Then he asked for more rope, evidently looking for a good place to stand and rest. But he took more and more rope and finally, after 30 feet of backing down, he stopped. I asked him what was going on. He replied, 'I am very hungry and want to eat something and rest.' After all, the last time we had eaten was at camp in the morning. Fifteen minutes later, he appeared again over the edge. Now he started catching hail stones that were coming down, explaining that he was thirsty.

"At this point, I was sure that we would not get to the top that day. We had lost a lot to time and were in the market for a good bivouac site. We decided to settle for a place to sit down for the night. Coming around one of the vertical ribs, I sighted a 50-foot chimney about three feet wide. This was my alley all right. With John belaying me I stemmed up and rested on the top of it on a narrow shoulder. In the beginning of the day that would have been a very easy thing, but by this time we all had to dig deeply into our reserve strength. John and Jack followed. Somewhat to the left, and a few yards up, I discovered a six by four foot hanging ledge. It did not take me long to decide that this was it. An open-air room with running water, that, as it turned out, ran down our backs throughout the night. When I suggested that we bivouac at this place, my partners were enthusiastic. That was good because, regardless, they had to accept it, for it was getting dark.

Morning sun hits the bivouac high on Monitor's East Face.

"We cleaned away the loose rocks along the wall and pushed them to the front of the ledge. Then we collected some rocks and built a semi-circle in which we placed our knapsacks and part of our rope, so we could sit on them. Two thin cracks on the wall gave us an excellent chance for driving in pitons, one on each side of the shelf. We tied in for the night. I wanted to make sure that neither of my partners would walk out on me during the night. It was 7:30 in the evening by now. We put on our extra clothes. Jack had a sweater and a windbreaker; John had a windbreaker and a rain jacket. I had a woolen shirt and a long raincoat that we shared and used as a bivouac sheet. It wasn't unbearably cold. Our only concern and worry was that the people at the camp below, especially Jack's wife and my wife, did not know what had happened to us.

"For supper we had sandwiches. We had more than enough. Even the half grapefruit we brought along lasted a long time. It had been knocked around in our knapsack all day long, half of its juice absorbed by the pack. During the night, Jack chewed on the rind. Still we had some for the next day. For dessert John gave us some candies, which partly satisfied our thirst. To cut down on extra weight, we had left our water behind.

"After 'wiggling' around for a while, we finally found the most comfortable, and the only possible, position to spend the night — sitting. Between 'wiggles' we pulled the raincoat back and forth, and tried to cover up those parts that were still exposed and cold. We even fell asleep. Once or twice we stood up for seventh-inning stretches and tried slightly different sitting positions. At one time I awakened to rain. Jack was happy about this. He was thirsty, very thirsty. 'Joe, we can suck the raincoat. There's water on it!' I was afraid he would eat the raincoat, too. My feet were plenty wet. I had the choice of covering my feet or my neck. I went for the neck. At one time as we were rearranging the raincoat, I dislodged quite a supply of water that had collected in the sleeve. Enough to have satisfied us all. But my already soaked feet got it. I then had a new idea. I placed Jack's felt hat beside me and hoped for more rain. It came, but somehow no water collected in the hat. We had some thunder and hail, but we did not shiver or feel very uncomfortable through the long night. Like the proverbial three monkeys, we were sitting, John on one end, I on the other and Jack right in the middle. In spite of my effort to be optimistic, I felt uncertain at this bivouac place.

"Finally the night broke. The horizon began to take on color. It was about five o'clock. By six we got a few rays of sun. We decided to wait till we got good and warm before the final assault of the wall. On the grassy slopes below us there were several hundred sheep being driven out of the valley by their shepherds. They were noisy, and we could not sleep any longer. Then we noticed that it was starting to cloud up. So, after taking a few pictures, we gathered our belongings and I extracted the pitons that had guarded us so faithfully during the night. We were on our way again.

"I climbed ahead. After a few feet, I had to resort to a piton. After a rope length it got real tough. There were two narrow ledges ahead of us that ran parallel and were about four feet apart. I climbed up on the higher one and looked over the situation. The ledge on which I was standing ran into a smooth, vertical wall. About nine feet above me there was a hand wide band that led to a V-shaped crack that went up 80 to 85 feet. It ended in an overhang that looked impossible. To get around it one would have to get out on the open face.

"I tried to get started by placing a rope sling and stepping up. Two tries and no luck. So I went down to the lower ledge to investigate. This looked even more hopeless. We could not sit here. That was sure. So I returned to my original position on the higher ledge and called my technical aid — John. Once more the human ladder came into operation.

"From now on we could not make any mistakes for we were being watched. Orrin Bonney and Hal Johnson had left camp early and were trying to find us with their field glasses. They had been unable to locate us during the bivouac. But after the sheep were gone and we started climbing and driving pitons, they heard us and soon saw us. When they were sure we were all right, they took word to camp and gave assurance to the larger group that was coming up for us.

"At this stage, I reached the most ticklish and most exposed climb of the whole wall. I left John's shoulder and started on the narrow band slowly but surely. I made a traverse of about twenty-five feet to reach the V-shaped corner that led straight up. I asked John for a piton and pulled it up on the rope. I drove it in as well as I could, for the place looked bad. I was afraid I was really going to test this piton at this point.

"I pushed myself up mostly by friction holds, but soon had to step onto the open face on account of the overhang. I was sixty feet above Jack at this time, and John was belaying me through two carabiners. The biggest foot and hand hold through this long stretch was not wider than 3/4th of an inch. It was all right as long as there was no slip. But in the case of an off balance move, they would have been useless. Up ahead I could see some wonderful door knob looking hand holds, but to get there, I had to climb almost on the coloration of the rock. On such a place, I found myself stretching for a tiny hand hold three inches too far. I tried to reach it several times but couldn't get it. I knew I had to make it, for it would have been impossible to climb back. I tried once again. This time it clicked. My new position enabled me to get better holds, and then it seemed that I had reached a virtual staircase. But I could not find a place for belaying my partners. I had to go ahead, and after practically using all of my 120 feet of rope, I reached a fairly good position.

"When I stopped and rested for a second, I heard my wife call up to me. She had been watching me for the last few minutes. I could hear her voice as clearly as if she had been just fifty feet away. I was glad she came up and was happy that the stretch above us was short and looked comparatively easy."

Fralick remembers that, "We were squarely in the center of the face. This entire upper wall appears absolutely impossible from below, even in the eyes of experienced climbers. Joe was as deadly serious as I've have ever seen him. He moved out to the end of the ledge, placed a piton and climbed a very few feet above it. What he saw was not inviting. He retreated to the ledge, looked far out to his right for another way and even dropped down several feet to a ledge below ours. From this spot, there was likewise no alternative, so Joe returned to our ledge and prepared for the toughest climbing in his long career.

"His lead from this point was the finest I have ever known a man to accomplish. To start, he placed another piton above the first one and tied a sling into it. Then, the sling and a shoulder stand on John enabled Joe to establish himself on the nearly vertical wall at a point from which he made an extremely delicate traverse to the left above our heads. After this traverse, he was completely out of sight, and John and I were aware of his progress only by watching his rope. For long moments we watched it hang motionless, and then with immense relief saw it begin to run out again after each such pause. We knew our leader so well that the painfully slow movement of the rope told of very great difficulties above.

"John and I exchanged frequent glances mixed with wonder and admiration, to which an element of concern was added as Joe gradually used up almost the entire length of the rope. In the upper part of this long lead, he really derived little or no effective protection from our belay or from the pitons he had placed along the way, because the amount of rope left to run out in the event of a slip was inadequate to absorb the shock of a fall from so far above. His great height was evidenced by the speed of the stones which he sent down. At first we could watch these, but later they whirred by unseen. Finally, after a very long time and after taking out practically the entire 120 feet of rope in this single lead, Joe found a place from which he could belay."

Returning to Joe's story, "John came up after me and took almost as much time as I did. I hoped that he would not slip. It would have been a bad place to find a starting position again. There was very little space where I stood, so when John reached a fairly safe place, I asked him to stop till I climbed to a much better belay position about 20 feet above. John finished this section and, standing where I had been, he pulled up our packs. Jack was still on the end of the rope, but in order to keep connection between him and me, I had to extend the nylon rope with the sling rope I had brought along.

"Now Jack started out and John belayed him. As soon as I had the nylon climbing rope in my hands, I shared the belay with John. On the way, Jack tried to extract as many pitons as he could, however, he had to leave some behind. Besides losing sling ropes and pitons on this part, Jack lost a piton hammer too. But I still had my hammer, and we got along well. There was just a little more to the finish. Thinking back on it, I don't think those 140 feet cost us as much strength as some of the other parts, but it was for me the most difficult. It had taken us around two hours to climb.

"There was just an easy stretch straight up and then we went into an easy gully, from which only one rope length separated us from the top. We looked down on the boulders where our friends were watching. As they started to move around, they looked like toy figures. They kept quiet as we started to climb our last section. I was going to use one more piton, but John kidded me about getting so particular all at once. I had just climbed worse rock without any. A few minutes before eleven I was practically in sight of the very top and yodeled our victory to our friends below. My partners came up shortly. And we shook hands. This mountain tried, but could not keep us."

Fralick remembers their arrival on the summit, "The last rope lengths were distinctly easier than the proceeding one, but the rock was looser than in any other part of the route. We climbed this final section with great care, realizing that now only an accident could alter the happy outcome of an issue which had exacted far greater efforts than any we had anticipated 26 hours earlier. At 11:30 a.m., the last man was up and the first ascent of the East Face was completed. The final 300 feet of the route had required four and a half hours.

"Our arrival on the summit ridge was the occasion for a chorus of yells and calls from the top of Peak 12. A group from the camp had watched our progress throughout the morning from points near the base and on Peak 12. They shouted long and loud, and we were very happy that the moment had arrived for calling back to them with equal enthusiasm. After building a little cairn on the ridge to mark the point where we had emerged from the face, we turned toward the summit, which was perhaps another 100 feet higher. On reaching the summit, Joe said to John Speck, 'Well, John, you will never climb it harder!' Then he turned to me, "Now, Jack, you have really done something.' But all we

(left to right) John Speck, Joe Stettner, and Jack Fralick after their 1947 climb on the East Face of Monitor Peak.

could do was sit down, rest, eat a little and simply enjoy being there. Just before descending, we entered our names in the register with the notation, 'August 9-10, 1947 Via East Face.'"

Joe took an accounting of the climb. "Out of the twelve pitons, we had only three left. We used them over and over again. We placed nineteen, the most I ever used on any climb before. We had three or four rope slings, and two shoulder stands. We lost a carabiner and a hammer. The skin of our fingers was all worn off. That and a few scratches here and there were the only signs of our struggle.

"When we returned to camp, there was quite a welcome. Our friends waited for us with flowers, and our good cook, John Walter, treated us with fresh apple pie and grapefruit juice. Cameras clicked and everyone was happy for one reason or another. But our wives were missing. To protest our adventure, they walked out on us. Well, they did not keep us in the dog house very long. They too were glad to see us back, although for a while they looked more threatening than Monitor itself."

Fralick adds some final thoughts about the climb and about Joe Stettner. "The East Face of Monitor Peak is an extremely difficult climb. Joe Stettner considers it to be the most difficult he ever accomplished — even more severe than either the Stettner Ledges route on the East Face of Longs Peak or the North Ridge of the Grand Teton. The difficulties are continuous, and they increase as height is gained — building up to two passages of the utmost severity: the 'lie-back-crack' and the '140-foot lead.'

"It is hoped that, between the lines of this recital of cracks, chimneys, ledges and overhangs, something of my admiration for my leader has emerged. Joe Stettner so magnificently conducted himself as leader that he instilled in us something of his own self-confidence and perhaps inspired in us a small part of his own great courage. To have been a companion of such a man on his greatest climb was a privilege which will occupy a niche in my mountaineering memories as commanding as our bivouac ledge high on the East Face of Monitor Peak."

The climb of Monitor attracted considerable attention, a very unusual situation for Joe. Fralick wrote about the climb in the December issue of *Trail and Timberline*. A member of the Chicago Mountaineering Club told a neighbor who was a writer about the daring adventure. The writer took great interest and wrote a feature article for the July 1951 issue of *SAGA, The Magazine of True Adventure*. Prominently displayed on the cover is an artist's sketch of Joe, decked in his ever-present stocking cap, holding on to a rope, as though he had some form of belay from above, and looking into the abyss with eyes filled with fear — the title: "Three Men On A Rope: Mountain Climbers Defy Death." Despite the silly title, the article was well written and widely distributed.

The 1951 cover of SAGA magazine with an artist's sketch depicting Joe in a worried state.

Godfrey and Chelton in their book, *Climb! Rock Climbing in Colorado,* wrote several pages about the Monitor climb. They concluded:

> The ascent of Stettners Ledges in 1927, the North Face of Lone Eagle in 1933, Joe's solo ascent of the East Face of Longs in 1936 and the East Face of Monitor in 1947, firmly established the Stettner brothers as the most daring and technically advanced rock climbers active in Colorado in the 1930s. Their climbs are all the more impressive when one remembers that their home was in Chicago and that their climbs were made on brief vacation visits to Colorado. Who knows what they might have accomplished had they lived closer to the high mountains?

In the 2000 edition of his book, *Roof of the Rockies, A History of Colorado Mountaineering,* William Bueler devoted five pages to the climb. He wrote:

> Fittingly, the first great rock climb of the post-war era was the work of Joe Stettner — the same climber who with his brother Paul had established the route on Stettner Ledges twenty years earlier. The 1,200-foot nearly vertical east face of Monitor Peak is the greatest wall in the Needles, and its first ascent in August 1947 by Joseph Stettner, John Speck and Jack Fralick was another real landmark in Colorado mountaineering history. This was the most sustained rock climb done in the state up to that time. While Longs' precipice was being assaulted in the 1950s and 1960s by an ever-growing army of rock climbers, the remote east face of Monitor was not climbed again until 1968 . . . The second ascent of the face, twenty-one years later, was made by members of a new generation of rock climbers, Larry Dalke and Paul Stettner Jr., Joe's nephew. The climbers began somewhat to the right of the 1947 route but joined the original route about 300 feet from the top . . . Though technically less demanding than some recent climbs of Longs and other peaks, the Monitor face remains one of the major rock climbs of Colorado. Larry Dalke, when interviewed by the authors of *Climb!* in 1975, said he had strong recollections of the technical difficulties and the rotten nature of the rock. "It's one of the few climbs I'd never want to repeat," he concluded.

How did Joe feel about all this publicity? "I always enjoyed it when people said I climb good," he said with typical modesty.

chapter 17

Inclusive policy in the club

I n spite of world-wide denouncement of the Nazis for
their anti-Semitism following the Second World War,
the sentiment thrived throughout the United States. In
Chicago, for example, Jews were not offered jobs in law firms or invited
to join country and social clubs. Many neighborhoods took special care
to discourage, and even to prevent Jews from buying homes and settling
there. To a considerable degree, this explains the existence of Jewish law
firms and country and social clubs of the immediate post-war era. It also
explains the existence of Jewish neighborhoods and communities in the
Chicago area. It is therefore not surprising that anti-Semitism made an
appearance in Chicago's mountaineering club.

It was several years after the Second World War. The soldiers
had returned, and the Chicago Mountaineering Club had made great
progress in attracting its old members and re-establishing itself. The Club
had already conducted a very successful Western Outing in 1946 with 38
members participating. Still, it hoped to increase its membership by
actively seeking people with a sincere interest in climbing and
mountaineering. And the club's membership grew. It was not long
before several Chicago-area Jews expressed an interest in the Club, which
inspired consternation and opposition from some club members.

In 1948, Joe had been elected president of the Club and in 1949,
was presiding over it when this controversy began to rip at the club's
fabric. Joe remembered the time well:

"It came to a head when two Jewish climbers applied for membership. They met our club's requirements. They had a sincere interest in the mountains and had climbed with the club a couple of times. There was no opposition to them personally.

"Paul and I were very opposed to this anti-Semitism. In fact, we were even opposed to discussions about race or politics or religion in club activities, and particularly to any decisions based on race or politics or religion.

"We had learned from our mother and father. My father said that people always think that Jews are cheating them. But he didn't believe this, and I didn't either. He always said that Jews are just as good as other persons. He thought they were smart people. He said that the people who criticize the Jews are unfair. He defended the Jews and often said that they were no different than anyone else. In Germany there was so much hatred of the Jews. My mother always said that you can get a fair deal from the Jews.

"There was a related side to this problem in the Club. At about this time, the editor of the Club's newsletter wanted to put a prayer and reference to Jesus Christ in the beginning of each edition. I was president of the Club then and just listened. But Paul was very opposed to this. He was strict about this kind of thing. 'This doesn't belong in the Chicago Mountaineering Club,' he said. Paul eventually prevailed. He also opposed starting meetings with a prayer, which some of the members wanted.

"You know, little by little, some people want this kind of thing to sneak in. I wanted to keep the mountains clean of this racism, religion and politics. In the mountains, this should play no role.

"Paul was more outspoken than I. I remember him becoming very angry with a woman who didn't want any Jews becoming members. She was a beast. I was the Club president and urged the Club to stop this. The membership eventually agreed with us.

"After that, the Club admitted several Jewish people to membership, including Walter March[34] and Stanley Kaplan, who later became a good friend of mine. Ever since that time, the Club has been open to all people who love the mountains and climbing. That's the only real requirement of membership. Paul and I were very proud of this."

Because of the brothers' strongly held beliefs about racism and anti-Semitism, and their firm and outspoken stand, the Chicago Mountaineering Club soon embraced their views and made them a part of its official policy. The Chicago Mountaineering Club became one of the first open-membership clubs in the Chicago area.

The Stettner boys apparently had not come to America to live with the racist and anti-Semitic attitudes from which they had escaped. The ideals of their father and the spirit of the Sektion Neuland of the German-Austrian Alpine Club had prevailed, at least in the Chicago Mountaineering Club.

chapter 18

Yodeling and Other Traditions

Nancy Robertson and I had just reached the summit of an inconspicuous peak in the San Juan Mountains of southwestern Colorado. She started flapping her arms up and down, in the fashion of a bandy rooster, and let out a wild howl that bore a vague resemblance to a yodel. Nancy, like many Chicago Mountaineering Club members of the time, had acquired the habit of yodeling to celebrate the reaching of a summit. Yodeling was not limited to summits. CMC literature reveals that the yodel was used to exchange greetings from afar, to indicate location, to indicate wrong direction or position, to indicate right direction or position, to wake others up, to express alarm, to express joy, and to reflect an amorous state, whether joyful or not. It was a multi-purpose yodel.

As we were hiking back to camp, I began to think about the derivation of the CMC yodeling tradition. It was started by Joe and Paul. This is not to suggest that the Stettner brothers yodeled in the style of Nancy. It is to suggest that they imparted more than just technical climbing skills. To illustrate the importance and variety of their contributions, a few tales told by their climbing companions follow:

On humor on the climb

Jack Fralick tells this story. "Joe Stettner and I set out one morning to climb Wiessners Crack on the West Bluff of Devils Lake. Joe led the short one pitch climb in typical Stettner style and soon disappeared over the top of the cliff, where he set up a belay. Now it was my turn to climb. I started up, but soon got an arm stuck so firmly in the crack that I couldn't get it out. Despite my best effort, I just could not extract my arm. Venting great frustration, I yelled up at Joe for assistance.

"Soon Joe's head appeared over the top, his chin cupped pensively in his hand and his elbow resting on the cliff's edge. 'Now, Jack,' Joe advised, 'put your left foot in your right shoe.'

"Unable to execute this maneuver, I continued to vent.

"'Vell, Jack,' Joe shouted down in his Germanic accent, 'I guess I vill just have to leave you there.'"

Joe's humor wasn't limited to the verbal. Rod Harris, an early CMC member, tells about how Joe and he found a large crack while exploring some crags. "It was far too wide to stem or chimney," Rod explained. "So we stood there wondering what to do with it. Joe then put both feet on one wall and both hands on the other wall. And up he went, climbing the crack in a nearly horizontal position. He looked like he was going to do a belly-flop to the rocks below. I laughed. But I was also amazed. I'd never seen anything like it.

"I also was with Joe and Paul, and observed Joe lead some climbs with Paul belaying. Joe would yell down to Paul, 'Paul, throw me a piton. Any size will work.' Then he would try to pound it in a rock crack. To my surprise, he was often successful."

On humor and fun at the campfire

Many members tell of Joe and Paul's love of singing and entertaining after climbs and at CMC campgrounds, wherever they might be. They sang, drank, played games and talked to and enjoyed everyone. They loved to laugh. It set a happy tone for years. Many expressed amazement at the number of songs in both German and English that they had memorized. Apparently the Stettner brothers neglected to inform their friends about all the practice they had singing with Naturfreunde, the German hiking club, that loved to drink and sing as much as to hike. A CMC favorite was the "Happy Wanderer," which Joe and Paul insisted on singing in both English and German:

> *I am a happy wanderer,*
> *Along the mountain path,*
> *And as I go I love to sing,*
> *My knapsack on my back.*

> *Vallerie, vallera, vallerie,*
> *Vallera ha ha ha ha ha ha,*
> *Vallerie, Vallera,*
> *My knapsack on my back.*

And so on. And then in German:

Mein Vater war ein Wandersmann,
Und mir steck'ts auch im Blut,
Drum wandr' ich flott, so Lang ich kann,
Und schwenke meinen Hut.

Faleri, falera, faleri
Falera ha ha ha ha ha ha,
Faleri, falera,
Und schwenke meinen Hut.

But Club lyricists felt compelled to improve the Stettners' favorite song. This new, improved version, was composed by Jennifer and Ron Angel, Ed Barts, Jim Hagan and Alice Eix, but was titled "The Happy Blunderer":

Joe is a happy blunderer,
Along the mountain track,
Every time he climbs a peak,
He's forced to bivouac!

Vallerie, vallera, vallerie,
Vallera ha ha ha ha ha ha,
Vallerie, Vallera,
He's forced to bivouac!

Paul always takes a compass,
To guide him safely back,
But he can't tell which end is north,
The white one or the black!

Chorus

We followed Joe to Lookout,
Until we became quite weak,
He built a cairn where we were,
That's how we made our peak!

Chorus

Paul led a climb up Uto,
The trip seemed awfully short,
They found themselves on Terminal,
And ended up in court!

Chorus

At an outing in the Tetons, Betty Alice Burns, author of the *1945 Iowa Mountaineer Report*, writes, "We sang songs around the campfire every night — mostly German songs in which Joe . . . sang the verses and we joined in on the chorus."

On the final night of a 1948 outing, Joe was in full glory. According to Gordon Goodrich, Joe entertained his fellow climbers "with a Russian sword dance, while the enthusiastic audience sang the Beer Barrel Polka . . . Joe was then given an honorary membership to the Iowa Mountaineers." He employed an ice ax, in lieu of a sword.

According to long-time club member Charlie Pierce, Paul liked to play a game he called "The Shoemaker," particularly with new CMC members whom he would select to be the shoemaker's apprentices. Of course, Paul was the shoemaker. As Charlie explains, "Paul would arrange three stools or logs in a row. He would be the shoemaker and sit on the middle stool. His apprentices would sit on each side. Paul would then take a shoe and lecture at length, and in boring detail, about the construction of the shoe. When an apprentice would lose interest and focus, Paul would whack him on the leg.

"To make the game more of a challenge for the apprentices, he equipped each apprentice with a stick to ward off his whacks. None was ever effective in defending against the master shoemaker's whacks. Paul would lecture, the apprentice would get glassy-eyed, Paul would quickly whack, and the apprentice would vainly swing the stick in defense. This game entertained club members for long periods."

Well, enough of Bavarian slap-stick.

on being dapper

In her 1945 outing report for the Iowa Mountaineers, Betty Alice Burns described Joe, "The outing personnel included members of the Chicago Mountaineering Club as well as those belonging to the Iowa Mountaineers. Joe Stettner acted as Chief Guide on the trip. He's quite the picturesque fella with his red cap, pack and ice ax, or at the campfire with his repertoire of German songs. His wife, Edith, runs him close competition for being full of fun, ambition and energy."

on physical conditioning

Many fellow climbers remarked about the standard of fitness the Stettners set for others to follow. They moved quickly and strongly. How did they maintain this physical fitness? Paul's son, Paul Jr., born on Christmas Day 1938, offers an explanation, "I remember going with Dad to Turnverein, a workers' gymnastics club, every Friday night, where we worked on calisthenics, on apparatus and high and parallel bars and played volley ball. Every third week we went to Devils Lake and climbed. We played Faustball, a German form of handball, every other weekend in Genoa City, Wisconsin, another German community. We went swimming and played soccer regularly. And we danced and went cross-country skiing and played hockey at Fox Lakes.

"My Uncle Joe didn't work out quite as much. But he also played Faustball, hiked with the Naturfreunde, climbed sand dunes in Indiana, danced, taught skiing to everyone he knew, played hockey and skied. He never ate much. And he participated in singing groups."

There is little indication that Joe or Paul made any particular effort to train and to "get into shape" for their climbing ventures. Their conditioning appears to be more a by-product of their love of a variety of sports. CMC member George Pokorny remembers one exception, "It was a very hot July day, probably in 1959. Paul, who was the outing chairman for the club's bi-annual Western Outing, scheduled for later that summer, must have begun to fret about the physical conditioning of club members. On this day, he selected four or five climbers, including me, for his climbing party. He immediately marched us up a long boulderfield. It was hot, humid, long, hard and exhausting climbing. When we reached the top of the boulderfield, we were beat, sweating and panting. We sat down, took out our water bottles and started drinking. Paul barked, 'All right, let's turn around and do it again. We need to get our legs in shape.'"

John Madsen, Joe's son-in-law, offers an emotional explanation for the Stettners' extraordinary mountaineering strength. "They had a great and remarkable passion for climbing and for the mountains. It possessed them. When they were there, this passion simply drove them on. That, I think, is the main explanation."

on teaching climbing and mountaineering

Joe enjoyed being a mountaineering teacher, as is clearly shown by the story of Joe's snow school in Wyoming's Wind River Range in 1948. According to Sue Schrader's report, titled *Mountaineering School:*

> About 30 Mountaineers . . . left camp at 11:00 a.m. for a practice session along the banks of Dinwoody Creek, about 45 minutes upstream. About half-way to the chosen snowfield, we paused while . . . Joe Stettner with purple shirt and red tasseled cap . . . showed us (and the movie camera) the correct and incorrect ways to guide a group over a difficult spot . . .

The group then went up the snow field, making quite a spectacular sight with some in shorts and T-shirts and others in wool sweaters and gloves and parkas, and all with ice-axes and big boots. Joe Stettner gave them instructions in falling down the snow field and catching themselves with their ice axes. He somersaulted down the snow field, caught himself, climbed back up to the group and then Edith Stettner, who was taking movies from the bottom of the snowfield would yell, "Do it again — I want another picture." Then he'd do it over again! Mickey Thomas was the sliding example for ice belay. Poor Mickey rolled down, was yanked to a stop by Joe, climbed back up to the group, and then the inevitable "Do it again" came from the bottom of the slope.

Joe gave instructions in knot-tying and crampon technique, cutting ice steps and glissading. He turned everyone loose, then, and the fun began! The slope was soon covered with sprawling, sliding individuals, trying their balance at glissading and punctuating their unsteady track every few feet with a "sitzmark." This continued until 4:00 p.m. Then part of the group left and the rest stayed for instruction in rappelling and practice in cutting ice steps. They returned later, but not too late for dinner, you will note.

And he urged his climbing partners to continue on, as explained by University of Iowa physical education professor Allen Wendler, "We finally hit some snow [on a route up Mount Adams] where we dug out our ice axes. Eight people wanted to drop out but after some encouragement from Joe Stettner . . . continued on."

All, however, was not adulation and praise. One aspirant climber, on her first venture to the crags, found herself assigned to a climbing party headed by Joe and Paul. She tells this story, still with fire in her eyes, about her attempted trip down a long boulderfield. It was at the end of the day, and she was tired and had had no experience on boulderfields. "It may have been a stroll for Joe and Paul, but it was terrible for me," she remembers. "I wanted to go back and find a more reasonable way, but they were pushy and yelled at me to come down. It frightened me to death. They acted like Prussians, and it made me miserable." This climber never developed a passion for climbing, but later learned to rappel and enjoyed it.

On doing new routes with young mountaineers

John Speck wrote this passage in the third person about his climb of Nez Perce in the Tetons in 1945:

During the early hours of August 24, the sky was filled with bumpy gray clouds, but by seven o'clock these had mostly cleared away . . . Joe and John waited in camp in hope that John Ebert might tear himself away from the luxuries of the valley and come up to climb.

Finally at about nine, Joe and John set off to climb Nez Perce, equipped with knapsacks, cameras, rope, pitons, etc. They hopped bounders up the canyon a short distance, then traversed the left shoulder below a prominent rock nose to reach a snow and ice filled gully extending up into the north face of Nez Perce. Since they were wearing only sneakers, they were forced to climb on the left wall of the couloir to avoid the ice, or sometimes they ascended the chimney between the rock and the ice. The upper portion was difficult because of the very fragile nature of the rocks. Joe took the rope up to the notch and belayed up the other climber carrying the two rucksacks. As it eventually turned out, the notch at the top of the gully was situated between the two lower eastern peaks of Nez Perce. A short vertical wall on the right led to some easy ledges extending around the south side of the larger east peak. These were reached at about noon.

Lured on by the easy going, the climbers passed several chimneys leading up toward the summit of the east peak. As a result they found themselves confronted with an overhanging wall on the southwest side of the east peak, near the notch between the east peak and the main summit to the west. Joe Stettner took the lead up this exposed wall. On the first pitch, he put in four pitons and took out over a hundred feet of rope before reaching a small ledge. Then he pulled up the rucksacks and belayed up the other climber, who was unable to find a comfortable position or resting place until Joe had left to climb the next pitch. The whole procedure was repeated two or three times, the interest sometimes being increased by the difficulty in throwing the rope down to the second climber. The summit of the east peak was reached at 4:00. The wall had provided some real climbing because of the exposure, overhangs, and occasionally scanty holds. Some time was spent on the summit eating lunch and photographing . . . A descent was made over easy ledges on the east ridge, until the north face could be traversed westward to the notch between the east peak and the main summit. Then easy ledges again led to the main summit . . . The climbers were greeted with kisses from Edith Stettner, who had returned from the valley, and with hot soup and other edibles.

Later, it was learned that this was a new route on Nez Perce. It is now rated Grade II, class 5.7, in Ortenburger & Jackson's *A Climber's Guide To The Teton Range.*

A study of Iowa Mountaineer and CMC club records reveals a number of these first ascents with relatively inexperienced mountaineers. A couple of examples: Joe, Edith and Fralick did a new route on North Thumb on the Needle Mountains Outing in the San Juans in 1947. In 1949, Paul took Al Philipp and Fralick with him on the first ascent of the North Corner of Hallelujah in the Big Horn Mountains of Wyoming. This turned out to be a very challenging climb, which today is rated Grade II, 5.6 or 7. Interestingly, Reinnie Mankau, Pete Pfister and Bill Primak, all members of the Chicago Mountaineering Club, climbed an equally challenging route up the West Face on the same day. It was a first ascent.

Also during that outing, Paul took Fralick, D. Johnson, P. Pfister, Philipp and Primak on a long route up the West Ridge of Black Tooth. This also was a first ascent.

On discovering practice climbing areas in the flatlands of the Midwest:

Joe and Paul were forever on the lookout for practice climbing areas. As mentioned earlier, they were likely, in 1926, the first to perceive Devils Lake as an excellent rock climbing practice area and climbing classroom. They invited their friends from Naturfreunde to climb "at the Lake." Now over 15,000 climbers pursue their passion for rock climbing each year at Devils Lake. On some days, as many as 300 cragsters are climbing there. From the perspective of the old timers, who had the Lake all to themselves, this is simply mind-boggling.

Joe at Devils Lake in 1949.

In the early 1940s, Joe got the idea of ice climbing at Starved Rock State Park in Illinois, an enchanting area with numerous ice falls that form in canyons along the Illinois River. Some of these ice falls are 80-feet high. A 1946 CMC newsletter reports:

> It was several years ago that Joe Stettner first mentioned Starved Rock Park as a possible location for a winter outing. This year he received such a good response that we decided to make the trip on February 4th.
>
> The day turned out to be better than we expected it. It was sunny, and although the air was nippy, it was comfortable throughout the day. There was hardly any snow on the ground, but the water-falls in the canyons were frozen solid.
>
> Our outing chairman [Joe himself] made a strong appeal to have everyone out by 9 o'clock so that we may have a full day of workout. He himself, however, did not show up till 12 o'clock or so. On the way he did not watch the road, and nearly landed in Peoria before he woke up to the fact that he was going in the wrong direction . . .
>
> In the afternoon, after Joe arrived, most of the group walked over to the Horseshoe Canyon, where our new member Wilfred Rall, was the first to tackle the water-fall. With a belay from below, he made it very well. A number of others followed him finding it an exciting hazardous problem, as a small amount of water trickled down the ice and soaked their clothes. Since most of us never had crampons on our feet, we found that secure feeling on ice very novel, and the trip was most worthwhile.
>
> On the way to our cars as the sun was slipping down, some of the fellows, who were still bursting from excess energy, started an impromptu hockey game on the mirror ice of the Illinois River. It was without skates, puck or hockey sticks, but with vigor and enthusiasm. Indeed our outing chairman was so badly broken up after the game that for a few days we did not know if he should not go in a hospital.

on action photography

John Ebert, director of the Iowa Mountaineers, wrote about Joe's enthusiasm for capturing mountaineering action on film, "The [1949] outing was photographed in 16mm color motion picture film by two experienced movie photographers. Joe Stettner carried his *Bolex* turret head camera with him and pranced around like a mountain goat getting action shots."

Joe also won a 1949 New York City photographic contest with one of his skiing photos.

Joe was an enthusiastic action photographer, including this shot of a skier.

On avoiding dry-mouth

Betty Burns, in her 1946 Iowa Mountaineer report, wrote about a remarkable, but generally unknown, secret method of avoiding dry-mouth on a climb. "Joe, our guide, told us to keep a prune seed in our mouths to keep from getting thirsty. So I cheerfully chewed one all the way up. It certainly got tasteless! We had some rope work, and I was a bit scared (I take that back — I was very scared) going up a chimney. And I almost swallowed my prune seed."

On organizing climbing festivals

In a 1977 testimonial, John Ebert of the Iowa Mountaineers noted that:

> [T]hrough the years Joe or Paul participated in many of the Iowa Mountaineer Summer outings, week-end outings, and frequently appeared as the featured speaker at our Annual Banquet. Between Joe and Paul, they served as climbing leaders on at least sixteen major outings or expeditions. Among the most important ones were: the 1948 Northern Wind Rivers Outing and the Devils Tower Group ascent; the 1949 Washington Cascade Outing; the 1951 Mount McKinley Expedition; the 1953 Bugaboo Outing; the 1955 Eastern Alaskan Range Expedition and many others. Generally their delightful mountaineer wives, Edith and Anne, accompanied them, and they too added something special to the outing.

CMC records show that Joe and Paul organized three Western Outings for the Club and led an innumerable number of climbs in the Midwest.

On mass ascents of Devils Tower

John Ebert wrote of Joe's role in the Iowa Mountaineers group
assault on Devils Tower:

> In 1948 the Iowa Mountaineers made their historic
> group ascent of Devils Tower. Seven months of endless red tape
> between Washington, Iowa City and the Park Headquarters finally
> ended with our receiving approval, which in later years benefited
> other groups. Sixteen members were accepted for the ascent
> which included many of the finest climbers in the country. As
> leader, I had to decide who would lead the first rope party and
> help to set-up belay positions and select the route which in places
> offered choices. I chose Joe.[35] The decision was a wise one as he
> always placed the interests of the majority over those of a few.
> This was especially important as I was filming the ascent and
> wanted to obtain pictures from the bottom before heading up
> myself. The plan also included pulling up sleeping bags, food and
> water for our overnight camp on the summit. The day was
> extremely warm and in places the rock was almost too hot to
> touch. But everything went like clockwork because of Joe's skillful
> climbing and following the plan in exact detail. Bringing up the
> members and over 400 pounds of camping equipment, food and
> water depended on teamwork. Joe was the ideal team member.

Cole Fisher of the Iowa Mountaineers wrote about both Joe's
climbing and his lead:

> The initial pitch is a finger and toe-jam crack, which leads
> to the base of a leaning column. This crack, while not really
> difficult, is tricky, since it requires a certain amount of probing and
> experimentation to get the right combination. Even Joe hesitated
> here for awhile, and he later said that he considered this pitch the
> most difficult. Having reached the base of the leaning column, the
> next stretch may be climbed by using the column as one side of a
> chimney, with the main body of the tower as the other side. This
> chimney is a not too difficult scramble . . . The pitch above this,
> about 80 feet in length, was climbable by using a column to the
> right and a fairly deep crack about three feet from it as the two
> sides of a chimney. Joe put one hand and one foot on each side
> and just walked on up, making it look ridiculously simple.

Later that year, Joe got the idea that the CMC ought to duplicate
the Iowa group's achievement the following summer. So, logically, he was

selected to organize and manage this ascent of the Club's program. Fralick wrote about this climb in the *Iowa Climber:*[36]

> [W]e gathered around one of the tables to make final plans for the climb. There was much to be discussed — ropes, hardware, water, cameras, etc. Each member of the climbing party was to carry a karabiner and a piece of sling rope for anchoring himself to a piton at the various belay points on the route. There was certain to be some congestion at these points, and so it was thought wise to apply this precaution to each man, whether he was merely waiting at the stance or actually belaying. Finally the flashlights were turned off and we crawled into our sleeping bags . . .
>
> A hurried breakfast in the pale dawn of August 13 preceded the hasty departure of the first party at 5 a.m. This party consisted of Joe Stettner (leader), Dick Dean, Andy Hennig, Charlie Beierwalt, Pete Pfister, Bill Primak, Groves Kilbourn, and the writer. We scrambled up the lower rocks of the Tower in a diagonal direction to reach the prominent south shoulder at the point where it merges into the nearly vertical columns which extend to the summit perhaps 600 ft. above. Just to the right of this point, the wall recedes to form a slight bay, similar to a very shallow couloir. In this section, the columns are shorter than elsewhere, and can be reached by climbing the cracks between the columns and the adjacent wall against which the columns stand. The Wiessner and Durrance routes make use of two separate systems of cracks, but both routes come out at the west end of a grassy bench along which one can walk for perhaps 100 yds. to a series of easier cracks leading to the summit. We followed the Durrance route, as have all parties with the single exception of Wiessner's . . . Briefly the difficulties are confined to the section of about 400 ft. between the top of the south shoulder and the west end of the bench. The first pitch, the "Leaning Column," is perhaps the most difficult, while the 80 ft. crack immediately above it is the longest and probably the most strenuous pitch of the whole climb.
>
> As we had anticipated, the extreme heat of this typical August day proved to be as serious a factor as the difficulties of the route. Despite the fact that most of us were in good condition as a result of our climbs in the Big Horns, the climbing on the Tower was very hard work in such heat. We arrived at each platform puffing and panting, and usually sought the comfort of the slight amount of shade afforded by the next crack while someone already on the platform obligingly belayed the following man. The members of the second party were probably denied even this slight protection from the sun. Several canteens were carried by both parties, but these were nearly empty when the summit was reached.

As morning progressed, it became apparent that we would be able to carry out our plan of making the entire ascent and descent in a single day. Despite the heat, good progress was being made and there was a minimum of crowding on the small platforms which served as belay stances. Joe Stettner, who had started up the "Leaning Column" at 5:45 a.m., reached the summit at 11:40 a.m.

The second party consisted of Paul Stettner (leader), Tony Maier, Reinnie Mankau, Max Eberli, Merritt Kastens, Al Philipp and Frank Lundal. Paul started up the "Leaning Column" at 8:15 A.M., and his entire party reached the summit by 1:30 p.m.

The summit register showed that we had made the eleventh ascent of the Devils Tower, excluding the ascents by the old ladder prior to 1937. Joe Stettner had made a special register tube for this occasion. It is a stainless steel tube on which the words "Chicago Mountaineering Club 1949" are engraved . . . At 5:15 p.m., Joe Stettner, last man in the descent, finished the final rappel.

Fralick wrote that a telephoto movie[37] was taken from the base of the Tower during the 1949 ascent. The movie, according to Fralick:

. . . makes Joe Stettner look like a spider as he stems up the full length of the Durrance Crack with no appreciable pause and without getting into the crack itself. It should be noted that Joe Stettner was then nearly 48 years old. How was this pitch regarded by climbers of a later generation? A clue can be found in the March-April [1971] issue of *Climbing* in which Dick Bird describes his ascent of the Durrance Route with two companions. The description in Dick Bird's account indicates that these latter-day experts resorted to jamming technique in climbing the Durrance Crack, no doubt an effective and safe procedure, but one lacking the elegance and beauty of stemming throughout.

On seizing the moment

Rod Harris, a long time CMC member tells of an incident at a CMC banquet several years ago. According to Rod, "A climber introduced his new girlfriend to Joe, who asked if she liked to climb. 'She doesn't climb yet,' the young man said. 'But she wants to learn next year.'

"'Don't let it pass you by,' Joe responded."

On being your mountaineering brother's keeper [38]

Felix Hagerman was with Joe and several other CMC members in the Abbot Pass Hut on Lefroy in the Canadian Rockies. The weather was awful and seemed only to worsen. Felix tells this story:[39]

I don't think anyone really cared [about the weather anymore.] We were content for the time just to sit . . . talking and listening to the wind. Certainly no one entertained any ideas of climbing under the existing conditions. The only disquieting note had been a report [that] . . . a party of two climbers were attempting Lefroy via one of the routes on the Victoria Glacier side of the mountain. Joe commented at the time that he hoped they made it down to the hut before evening, otherwise we'd have to go looking for them. Since we couldn't even see Lefroy from the hut, that wasn't too pleasant a prospect.

We went out of the hut for a little air . . . It was then that we heard the first yodels. We called back and the exchange was repeated . . . It was evident they needed some bearings. And, as this was the case, Joe said we'd better go take a look. If there was ever a figurative statement, this was it, as once above the hut, visibility was about as near zero as it ever gets in the daytime.

We left the hut and proceeded straight up [talus and] up the snow . . . It was impossible to see anything and once on the mountain we could no longer hear anything. To further complicate things, the party above quit yodeling. This made it appear hopeless. Joe thought they might have gone back to try to descend their original route. This seemed logical and . . . the storm was getting much worse. We decided to think about getting down ourselves. In due time, we reached the hut again; cold, wet, and still concerned over the welfare of the unknown climbers somewhere above us in the clouds. By now it was mid-afternoon.

I'd just taken my boots off and my feet were well ensconced in the oven when the yodels started again. They sounded nearer. Joe immediately started up again and went as far as the tongue of talus. I put my boots on again. [One of our group] called, "I see 'em." He was right. A hole had opened in the clouds and there, still high up, were two dots moving in the clouds and very slowly downward. We were very glad to see them, but their location was rather disturbing. They were much too far to the left . . . Below them the slope steadily steepened until it dropped off almost vertically to the Victoria Glacier. The whole area was streaked with avalanche tracks. A traverse back to the west was possible provided it was made before they got below the cliff band. Below that it would be well nigh impossible. They obviously had not been above to see either the pass or the hut and, being unfamiliar with this side of the mountain and, naturally, disoriented because of the storm, were off route. We found later that two rappels had been necessary to cross the cliff bands above where we saw them . . .

We decided the best bet was to cut up and across in an attempt to intercept them above the black cliffs. We set out. Once more the storm was with us and we moved in a swirling world of white entirely cut off from everything and only memory as a guide. Time was important, not only because of the lateness of the day, but because we had to establish contact, either verbal or visual, before the others were too low.

As soon as we moved to the left of the route, the snow began to steepen. Here, for the first time, the fresh snow became a problem. In some places, it was knee deep and here Joe would warn to "step easy." He was moving like a machine. Scrape with the ax, swing and kick, in with the shaft and step up. We could see nothing and hear nothing but the howling of the wind. A band of rock loomed up ahead and we tried it. Covered with verglas and snow, it was worse than the snow. Back to the slope. Another band. We cut up along side it. Now the angle grew so steep that handholds had to be cut. The new snow grew deeper as we went up. Another traverse across an even steeper slope lay ahead. Still no sign of the climbers.

By this time, I was beginning to get used to this "fly on a wall" feeling, especially since Joe didn't seem to be concerned. I was never worried about staying on the snow, but I was worried about the snow staying on the mountain. We were about in the middle of the slope in question and I was waiting while Joe tried to find a crust under a band of powder when with a shudder the whole surface shifted. I nearly jumped off the mountain. Joe didn't seem to notice.

"Joe . . ."

"What?"

"It moved!"

"What moved?"

"The whole works!"

"That's OK. We got work to do. Besides, the rocks hold it."

And off we went again. This not unassailable bit of logic at least had the effect of giving me something to do. I started trying to see where the rocks were that were doing the holding. I couldn't find 'em, but by this time we were over half way across and going on was as safe as going back. Besides, I reflected, it probably wouldn't hurt too long. And Joe was right, of course. There was work to do.

Once across this "restless" area, we had to cut up again. Still no sign and then we heard them. Not fifty yards to the left. We called and started traversing again.

We didn't know who it was, of course, and Joe suggested

that since we could tell one of them was a woman there might be some chance of panic and that we treat the whole thing as if it were "like a little afternoon exercise, be cheerful." I tried to comply by whistling, but all I could think of was "Pretty Redwing," which hardly seemed appropriate. Anyway, my mouth was too dry. As it proved, we could have saved our worries on that score. The climbers turned out to be Mr. and Mrs. [John] Mendenhall, not unknown in the world of mountaineering[40] and definitely not the panicky type. They were lost and, after fourteen hours of steady climbing in the teeth of the storm, very tired. However, they were still moving competently and safely. They had already shown exceptional skill and endurance and had they been able to see the pass, there would have been no difficulty. As it was, I think it would have been impossible for them to reach it safely. They knew Joe, of course, and some hand shaking was done while balancing in the driving snow. Then we started down with myself going first, to, as they say downstate, "holler fur the puddles." Joe came last, belaying the other two, and moving as calmly as if he were on Michigan Avenue. But as far as I was concerned, it was a mess. Visibility was absolutely zero and steps were filled with new snow and invisible.

On friendships forged in the mountains

By 1951, business had called Fralick away from Chicago. He could no longer regularly participate in CMC activities. But it did not break the bonds of friendship. Many years later, Fralick visited Joe at his home. The day is vivid in Jack's memory. "When Joe saw me, he remarked, 'Yes, Jack, the rope is still there.' I have never heard words that have had more meaning to me."

That this bond was never broken is clear from Joe's letter to Fralick.

Chicago Nov. 22, 77
Dear Jack,

A few days ago I got several copies of the new issue of *The Chicago Mountaineer.* Again you have built for the Stettners a pedestal to put them on. For me, as ever, your article is interesting, but it is not necessary to give so much credit to us. We climbed mountains only for the sport and enjoyment of it. I appreciate the honor you give us, but sometimes it has to slow down.

Dear Jack, in one way I understand your feelings toward us. We have gone through some interesting experiences together

Joe at age 63.

which don't occur often in every one's life. We have been roped together on climbs in serious situations, and it seems to me this rope is still on even if it is invisible. In my mind, it will stay on forever. So, Jack, I am glad we met on grounds we both enjoyed so much.

As ever in friendship,

Joe

In these ways, Joe and Paul shared their passion and their lives.

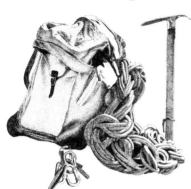

chapter 19 Accidents and Tragedies

"I wasn't that smart," Joe reported when I asked him about accidents on his climbs. "Just lucky that nothing serious ever happened on my climbs. Luckily I got away with some things. There was never a close call. No one was ever killed. And so I got away with it, since I am not doing any more climbing."

Joe's attribution of his accident-free climbing career to good fortune hardly explains this phenomenon. In spite of his talk and, perhaps, his modesty, there were close calls. He caught Paul a number of times, particularly on their Rock of Ages climb in the Tetons. These "catches," however, were most likely a consequence of sound, safe belaying practices.

Much more revealing are two other incidents. The first, in 1941, involved Paul's dramatic 54-foot fall off Devil's Monument at Camp Douglas in Wisconsin. As discussed earlier, Joe, Paul and Fralick had completed a new route over some overhanging sandstone ledges. They were descending. Joe and Fralick, who was belaying Paul, were on a ledge, and Paul was descending to this ledge. Paul slipped when a handhold broke and fell. The force was great, pulling Fralick off his belay stance. He was pulled about six feet to the edge of the ledge. This had all the makings of a great tragedy. Everyone was in great danger. But nothing serious happened. Joe, during the whole incident, was backing up Fralick, and thus was able to stop both of them from falling to their deaths.

The second incident was very similar. It also involved Fralick. On the climb of the East Face of Monitor Peak, Fralick was belaying John Speck. Speck fell, pulling Fralick off his stance. Here again was a situation that seemed likely to lead to a serious tragedy. It did not happen. Again, Joe, from his higher position, had backed up Fralick's belay with his own.

These results were not a matter of luck. More accurately, serious injuries, if not multiple deaths, were avoided by Joe's mountaineering judgment and routine, safe mountaineering practices. So, his "good luck" explanation tells neither the accurate nor the entire story.

"I always tried to climb it safe," Joe concedes. "When I was at home, I often thought about climbing problems and how to solve them. For example, what if a climber falls over an overhang and is just hanging in mid-air? How does he get out of that jam? Most of these problems never occurred, but when one did, I had often worked out some solution in my mind that I could try.

"I also tried to anticipate problems. That's what I did on the Camp Douglas and Monitor climbs. I just backed up the belayer.

"When I went climbing with others, I taught everyone that, when they were standing on a ledge, they must put in a piton or some kind of protection and tie themselves to it with a sling. It's just a precaution. I always tried to make sure that my fellow climbers were capable. Usually nothing happened, and all the precautions were unnecessary. But sometimes, something does happen.

"That's what happened to John Speck. I liked him very much as a good friend. He was a smart fellow, and he was a good climber. I always felt he liked me too. He shouldn't have died. But John was not over anxious about something happening to him. I had taught him never to stand on a ledge without protection."

Speck was a young biologist and research scientist at the University of Chicago. He and another young member of the CMC, Graham McNear, were climbing on the Aiguille du Geant on Mont Blanc in Northern Italy in August 1949.

Joe seemed upset about the tragedy nearly 50 years later. "John was capable of leading. But McNear was a fireeater. He was young and didn't need experience or technique. They were by themselves and McNear was leading. Speck was below. McNear drove two pitons. Then he fell. The second piton pulled out and the first one didn't hold. He fell on John Speck and took him down. They fell down the face. Both were killed. John had not tied in like I had told him.

"I was with the Iowa Mountaineers when this happened. I got a telegram that John Speck was killed. John Ebert [director of the Iowa

John Speck, shown in the Wind River Mountains in 1946.

Mountaineers] was also upset. He liked Speck too. I just couldn't believe it. In some ways, I still can't.[41]

"A person was killed on one of Paul's climbs, and another was killed on one of his outings. In the Tetons, at a CMC outing in 1948, Paul and his group had just climbed the Middle Teton and were coming down in the dark late at night, and had reached the ice field a couple of thousand feet below the summit of the peak. Except for Paul, they were all beginners.

"The group had gotten spread out. They were not staying in line. One of the newcomers was climbing above the others. Arthur Tielsch was at the head of the group and lower. He was a friend of Paul's from his gymnastics club. The newcomer apparently slipped, fell and bumped into Tielsch, who lost his footing. He slid about 300 feet into the rocks at the bottom of the ice field, hit his head and was killed right there. By midnight, I'm certain that the snow was frozen and hard.

"His wife Olga was there. She and the others took his body to Salt Lake City for cremation. Edmund Lowe, who was a CMC member, gave a sermon.

"Paul was very upset about this accident, even angry. He thought that people who climb ought to know what to do. But that isn't always the case. People have to learn. Sometimes someone just loses his balance or something. Everyone should have a second trial, but without protection there is often no second trial. And accidents happen. If you don't protect, you may have to pay for it. Mountaineering is dangerous. You don't have to be a hero.

"Perhaps that is what Walter Kiener was doing when Agnes Vaille got killed." Joe's reference is to the famous Agnes Vaille tragedy on Longs Peak on January 12, 1925. Agnes was from a prominent Denver family and a member of the Colorado Mountain Club. She prevailed upon Kiener to take her up his namesake Kieners Route in the winter, thus achieving the first winter ascent of the East Face of Longs Peak. Agnes fell on the descent, and, totally exhausted if not injured, she was unable to continue. Kiener went on to get help. When he returned, Agnes was dead. A shelter near the Keyhole on Longs' tourist route has been erected in her memory, and in memory of Herbert Sortland, who died in an effort to rescue her.

"I've known Walter Kiener ever since climbing the Stettner Ledges. He found out about it from Charley Hewes and came to see Paul and I when we were at Bear Lake.

"Kiener, I think, made a lot of mistakes. He got far too late of a start. He and Agnes had started out three times before that winter and turned back each time. This time, in spite of unstable weather early in the morning, they decided to do it. It turned out that this was one of the worst days to do it.

"On one of their earlier attempts, Kiener lost his ice ax. A climber should not do that. On another occasion, when Alexanders Chimney was icy, he thought it was too dangerous, so he untied his rope, supposedly to save Agnes if he fell. He didn't want to fall and pull Agnes down. This makes little sense to me. The leader should use the rope to protect the second climber. This too strikes me as strange.

"What is most strange is that, even though Agnes had fallen several times on the way down and was exhausted, Walter did not have her on belay when they were coming down the steep North Face. Agnes could hardly move, and Kiener wasn't belaying her. I don't understand him. It was stupid. He didn't have all cylinders going. That's when she took her long, last fall. I lost a lot of respect for Kiener as a climber and a guide when I learned this."

"How do you know about this, Joe," I asked.

"Walter told me some things. Charley Hewes told me some things. But Kiener told Charley most of these things and Charley wrote

Agnes Vaille in the 1920s. (Courtesy the Colorado Mountain Club)

it down. You don't know about that?" Joe was surprised and explained.

"After Charley died, his old desk was sold in an auction. The buyer found this old letter in back of a drawer in the desk. He gave it to Herb Keishold, who knew Paul and Anne [Stettner] through the CMC. Anne typed it up and made several copies. I've got one of them. You can have it.

"Kiener was infatuated with Agnes. She was a society woman who wanted glory. Walter was emotionally ruled by Agnes. He was mentally captivated by her. He let her push him into making climbing decisions that he should not make as a Swiss guide. And he paid for it all his life.

"Once, I had a similar situation. Morgan Perron wanted me to take her up Stettner Ledges. I said, 'No. Don't ask me.' I could take anything up, even a sack of potatoes. But I want to climb with someone who can really climb.

"It is true that Walter and Agnes made it to the summit. But Agnes was so shot that she couldn't finish. She couldn't finish the climb by getting back. She must have felt like I do now. I can hardly take another step. Mountaineering is too dangerous to make these kinds of judgments.

"Once, when Paul and I were in Glacier Park, we saw a Swiss guide taking eight people on a glacier. He was holding the rope in his hand. I said to him, 'Do you always do this?' Don't depend on something that is no good. It may be better to have no belay than a bad one.

Joe and Paul around 1960.

"You can't be soft if you are a guide. On Warbonnet in the Wind Rivers, an acquaintance of Paul's, a guy named Bollinger, fell to his death. He slipped right out of the rope and was killed. Bollinger was from Europe and supposedly had a lot of experience.[42] Paul never questioned him about how good he was.

"Paul may have been too lenient. He didn't want to be a schoolmaster. But sometimes you have to be.

"When I was the climbing chairman on our outings, I always insisted that everyone who went out of camp had to check in with me. I wanted to know who was going to lead. And I wanted to know that they had returned.

"Maybe I was too strict. I bawled out some climbers for not following these rules. But no one got badly hurt.

"I have thought a lot about these accidents. The way we climbed then had a built-in weakness. There were often three climbers. The first man should be in charge and the middle man was usually the weakest of the three. But it is this middle man who was actually responsible for holding the first and the third man. I sensed there was something unsafe about having the weakest climber protecting the stronger climbers. This problem became clear to me a long time ago. So I decided to always try to back up the middle man. That's what happened at Camp Douglas and on Monitor. I guess it was simply an attitude of safety and a desire to back up other climbers.

"You want to know how I developed that attitude? I've thought about that too. There's not much else I can do now but sit in my chair and think about things. As I've told you, Paul was really a better rock climber than I was. So it wasn't long before he started to do the majority of leading on rock. And he was bold. He was terrific with his toe-nail and finger-nail climbing.

"This worried me. I was nearly five years older, and from the beginning, I felt responsible for him. I had the feeling that I had to take care of Paul. So I was always preparing for and expecting a fall. Several times that happened, and I caught him. Paul really relied on me. I had this feeling from the very beginning of our climbing days back in Germany. I suspect that's how my attitude about safety began. I was taking care of my little brother. So many times I said, 'Paul, you do it. You know who is behind you.'

"But still, Jack, I was lucky and got away with some things."[43]

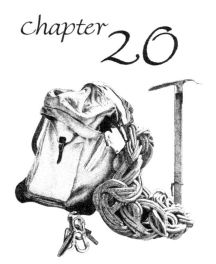

chapter 20

Joe in his Last Years

*A*fter a day of skiing in the Snowy Mountain Range near Laramie, my son Schani and I pulled our car in front of Joe's home. We were in a mild snow storm. When we reached the front door, we could see Joe snoozing in his chair. As I opened up the front door, he awoke. "Did you guys have a good mountain day?" he asked.

We assured him that we had — new powder snow, wonderful.

"That's good," Joe responded distantly. "You know, Jack, I've been sitting here all afternoon thinking about you, about skiing down white snow slopes and through the forests. I wanted to go skiing with you, through all the open spaces and trees. I wanted to go along. I'm jealous that I'm not doing it. You have so much pep, and I have nothing left.

"My doctor says I'm not sick. He says I'm just getting old. Edith's mother was 96, and she often complained about being tired and hurting. I always said, 'You're OK.' Now I'm the one who needs a kick in the pants.

"I really gave up climbing when I was about 57 or 58. So it's been a long time.[44]

"In 1977, young Paul [Paul's son] made plans to climb the Stettner Ledges on the 50th Anniversary of the climb. He wanted Paul and me to come along. It was just a stunt. Edith saw it right away as a stunt. Edith was angry with young Paul."

Joe's story brought to mind my own memories of this climb. Young Paul was an excellent climber and dreamed of a golden anniversary climb of the Ledges, featuring his dad, his uncle Joe and himself. It was a grand idea, full of boldness and fun, assuming the two older, vigorous gentlemen were still capable of climbing at that level.

I was in Estes Park that Summer and heard rumors of the climb. "Can you believe it! Joe and Paul Stettner are going to repeat their climb of the Ledges. Those guys must be in their seventies or older! Are they nuts or what?" That was the scuttlebutt. I don't know how the rumor got started. But it did. And it was making the rounds of the Estes Park climbing community.

When I returned to Chicago, I asked Joe about this. He acknowledged that such plans did exist and implied that he planned to do it. I had climbed the Ledges a year or so before and had vivid memories of a sustained, hard and challenging route. Siding with the Estes Park scuttlebutt, I thought, "How could a 76 year old guy do it? But then Paul and Joe had been great climbers. Perhaps they still are. And I am not. So maybe I ought not be so skeptical."

Several weeks later, I again saw Joe. I inquired about how plans for the golden anniversary climb were working out. "Not going," he reported, his head drooping a little. "Edith told me that if I try to do this climb, she'd divorce me." He seemed upset about the idea.

"She'd do that? Make you choose between climbing and her?"

"That's what she said," Joe answered. "And I think she is serious."

I walked away thinking, "Good for Edith. She is so sensitive and loving. Here she is, being the bad guy, but allowing Joe to back out of the climb and save face at the same time. She gave him a noble excuse." I also sensed that, on a level deeper than casual conversation between friends usually takes, Joe probably was thankful for her magnanimous gift.

Now 20 years later, Joe was talking more candidly about the matter. "Edith told me that, if I went on the climb, she wouldn't be there when I came home. Young Paul had worked on me and nearly talked me into going. But then I thought, If I can climb this thing 50 years later when I'm 76, people will start thinking that it wasn't that hard in the first place.[45]

"You know, I think maybe I could have done it. After all, I climbed Monitor when I was 46." When I pointed out that there is a significant difference between 46 and 76, Joe quipped, "Maybe for you! But I'm glad I didn't go. They didn't get too far. It rained and snowed, and they got sick.[46] And during the whole time, I was warm, and I was comfortable in my bed.

"I think about going climbing again now and then, but I know I can't. Several years after the Stettner Ledges anniversary climb, in the early 80s, I went to Devils Lake with my grandchildren to teach them a little about climbing. I tied a rope around their waists. It was a top rope. And I was going to belay them while they climbed up an easy part. One of my grandchildren began to climb. He was doing all right and was gradually moving up.

"As I was standing there watching him with my brake hand on the rope, I was overcome by this strange feeling that my hands were no longer strong enough to hold the rope if he fell. This struck terror in me. I told him to come down, and he did. No one was hurt, but I knew, at that moment, that my climbing was over. I couldn't take that risk with my grandchildren, or with anyone else."

Joe's post climbing days have brought a number of accolades, from the CMC which devoted its September 1977 publication *The Chicago Mountaineer* to Joe and Paul, from the American Alpine Club and from the Wyoming Alpine Club.

In the summer of 1996, a luncheon was held in Joe's honor at the Aspen Lodge which sits at the foot of Longs Peak. When Joe arrived, he climbed out of the passenger seat by placing his right hand above the door and, in a slick and effective but slow climbing move, stood up. This was not the kind of move older people make. Joe was climbing out of an alcove on the face of a big climb. In some ways, his climbing days will never end.

After dinner in Laramie that cold snowy day, Joe began to expound on his thoughts. He started to talk again about the 50th anniversary climb of the Stettner Ledges and Edith's hostility to it all. But soon his thoughts were really on Edith and life and death, particularly Edith's death. "When I came home and found Edith there, I knew she was gone. She had had a heart attack. It had to have happened fast, seconds maybe. The click of a clock. I'm happy about that. The clock clicked, then she was gone. It was all over then.

"I don't believe in ghosts and things like that. When I walk by pictures of Edith, I think of her, and in this way, she lives. If Edith lives, it is in my mind. She lives in my mind and in my heart. But when I die, she'll be gone from there, too. We'll then die together. There's nothing after death, nothing. I accept that. There is no reason to believe we will see each other again.

"I understand about this hope of an afterlife. You die, and a few minutes later, you see your old friends around the corner. But that just isn't true. It would be nice, but there is no truth to this.

"I don't understand why people don't see this — even very educated people. A friend believes that he has actually seen his dead wife

Joe and Edith at Devils Lake.

come around him. We have discussed this. But it is all in his mind. It is not reality. Some organizations take advantage of this hope. They say, give me $10,000 and you'll be able to see your loved ones again. This is a business, and it's not based on reality.

"You see, it is like a dream. You can dream and have a beautiful dream. But then you awake and the dream disappears. Nothing stays the same. Things always change. Edith had to die, I have to die, and you have to die. Everyone does. At that point, for each of us, it is all over. The dream is over.

"I'm glad that Edith did not suffer much. It is awful when someone is in the hospital, very sick and with relatives standing around and holding the sick person's hand. 'Is she dead yet?' 'No,' someone whispers, 'not yet.' It can go on and on.

"I don't want that to happen to me. If I die, I die, and it's all over. I am ready to die now. Perhaps tonight. But I don't want to go yet. I sit here most of the day and think about things. I can't really do much else. But I've learned a lot.

"The loss of my little brother Paul was very hard. He was almost five years younger. He should be here with me. We should be together. I miss him. But the loss of Edith has been even harder.

"If I hadn't have been so happy with Edith, it wouldn't have hurt so much. Still it's better to love a lot. When Edith died, I didn't really want to live. But I did, and I learned that I can take it. I can take even this. I know that I can take the most pain that life has to give. I got through the winter after my loss of Edith. I've taken it. One day, maybe I won't feel like getting up. But now I want to live. I've had a good life. I did everything I liked. It all came easy. Now here I am, in Laramie, with Ginnie and others I love. It's been good, although I don't have any pep. I don't ever want to go to an old folks home. This is a good place. I'm happy here.

"Nothing is forever. If something hurts you, it is not forever. If something is beautiful, it is not forever. Nothing is ever the same. It is always changing. Edith could not be here with me forever. I've experienced this great loss, I've taken it, and I've lived. That's really what I want, to live life fully.

"Now Jack, that's my sermon."

chapter 21

"We're Going Mountaineering"

I hadn't seen Joe for over six months. When he left Chicago, I was in Mexico pursuing our commonly shared passion. I was sorry that I wasn't available to see him off and to wish him well. I often wondered how he was handling the loss of his Edith and how he was adjusting to his new home.

What a minor shock it must be, I thought, to move from major cities like Munich and Chicago, where he had spent the 94 years of his life, to Laramie.

The directions to his new home were remarkably simple and straight forward. "Drive right into town. Keep going through a couple of lights to Grand. Turn right and go to 19th. Turn right again, go two blocks and stop." That isn't the way it is in Chicago. I followed these directions and found myself next to the Wyoming Cowboys football stadium. Joe almost lives on campus.

His new home is a modest, two-story place with a backboard for hoops playing and a nice little garden on the side for beer drinking, philosophizing and telling tall tales about climbing. There is a large city park a half block away. Very nice and tranquil, like my little hometown many years away, I thought.

As I walked up the sidewalk, Joe's daughter greeted me. Together we went into his living room. There, over the fireplace, was his wonderful copperwork of the Chicago skyline. Above the desk, he had placed his striking, large black and white photograph of the East Face of Longs Peak. Every time I see the East Face or a photo of it I seek out the Stettner Ledges and Joe's Solo. There they were. My eyes had become

Joe working on his copperwork.

very well trained. These works gave me the strange feeling of being in his home in Chicago — a form of *deja vu*, perhaps.

A few minutes later, Joe walked in, aided in his balance with his cane. He looked good. He was doing well with his loss and with Laramie. Ginnie, her children and Laramie apparently were good for Joe. He was even spunky, scolding me for my lack of punctuality. This character flaw had deprived us of a long afternoon together. Joe had retained his sense of *Punktlichkeit*.

I told him that I had many questions about his earlier years and several other matters to talk about. These matters can wait, he assured me. He wanted to show me his new home and to have a beer in his garden. Then, he said, we could go out to dinner. But most importantly, he wanted to tell me about the next day's plans.

"We're going mountaineering tomorrow morning. I'll bet you've never been to the Snowy Mountain Range, have you? We're going there tomorrow morning." There was excitement in his voice. I knew he was serious. Story telling would have to wait, I concluded.

The next morning, he insisted we eat a good, hearty breakfast of eggs, toast and coffee. "I have trouble keeping the egg shells out of the eggs," he complained as he worked hard to crack the eggs on his skillet. "But we need a good breakfast for the climb."

By mid-morning we were on our way, driving west of Laramie for about 40 or 50 miles. Gradually we gained elevation. Soon, we arrived at Lake Marie, at about 10,000 feet. Joe directed me to park in a little lot near the lake and the trail head.

Joe got out of the car and started up the path around the lake. Above us towered the gray, broken, snowy peaks of the Snowy Mountain Range. Joe looked up at these mountains as he slowly worked his way down the path. We talked about a couple of possible new routes up the wall across from the lake. Perhaps they haven't been climbed yet. This was Joe's world.

After a while, it became obvious that Joe was too tired to continue much further. So we retreated back to the car. He was exhausted, but

Joe in the Snowy Mountains with the author.

very pleased with his performance. "We should hurry to a restaurant I know where they have buffalo steaks," he suggested. "Do you like buffalo?"

We hurried off, stopping only to decide if we could see Longs Peak in the distance. We decided we could. Was it a hundred miles away? We wondered. Though our hunger was growing, Joe wanted to take a winding, out-of-the-way back road where the mountain scenery promised to be particularly striking. The road kept its promise. Eventually we made it to the restaurant.

That evening he fell asleep in his chair. His climb had been hard on him. The old mountaineer was exhausted. He slept late the next morning. Perhaps he had been too ambitious. Perhaps this had been too much for him, I thought. I left for a while to go running through Laramie.

Upon my return I found Joe sitting in his chair in the living room. "Where have you been?" he asked. "I've been up for quite a while." Without waiting for an answer, he muttered, "I'll fix breakfast." And he started to get up.

"You know, Jack, I climbed at 10,000 feet yesterday. And if I can climb at 10,000 feet, I don't need this cane." He stood up, threw his cane aside and wobbled across the living room on his way to the kitchen. "I'm not too steady any more, Jack, but if I can climb at 10,000 feet, I don't need a cane."

That's Joe Stettner as I remember him.

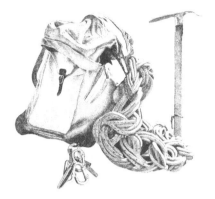

chapter *22*   *The End*

"*Do you know, Jack, I've told you many things about my life, perhaps more than I've told anyone. But there are some things I'm not going to tell. No one tells everything.*"

— Joe Stettner to the author in 1996

J oe Stettner died at the age of 95 on March 14, 1997. In an obituary for the *American Alpine Club Journal,* Jack Fralick wrote:

> With the passing of Joe Stettner at age 95 on March 14, 1997, we must acknowledge the loss of one of the most remarkable figures in American mountaineering history. Joe and his inseparable younger brother, Paul, who predeceased him on May 26, 1994, were at the forefront of the great climbers of their time. But they deserve to be remembered for more than their incredible skill. Their strength of character, devotion to their companions and love of the mountain world are the Stettner hallmarks that will be remembered longer than their climbing accomplishments. Indeed, they eluded recognition and fame during the early years of their careers, and became virtually legendary figures.

Appendix

Believed to be
Joe, in the
Austrian Alps.

Footnotes

Joe on the East Face of Longs Peak, probably in 1942.

1. See *The Chicago Mountaineer*, Vol. 30, No. 1, July-September 1977, pp. 3 - 12.

2. *"Edith is no longer."*

3. Flood, *Hitler, His Path To Power*, p. 37.

4. Craig, *Germany 1866-1945*, p. 460.

5. Flood, *Hitler, The Path To Power*, p. 38.

6. This "device" was not their only mountaineering innovation. Joe made a "big bro" type of protection for large cracks. This included two concentric tubes that could be expanded to fit in large cracks. They made many of their own pitons and were likely the first to use carabiners in America, as will be explained in Chapter 7.

7. The author/translator of this phrase had trouble rendering " . . . *getsda graisle"* into any form of English. When I asked Joe, nearly 70 years later, what it meant, he muttered something about "sacraments."

8. Paul (who was the lead climber) snapped a carabiner into the eyelet of each of these pitons and then clipped the climbing rope into the carabiner. See the Glossary for information on these devices and their use. Joe and Paul had ordered the pitons and carabiners from Munich and they arrived just before they departed Chicago. The carabiners are climbing tools that evolved from pear-shaped *Karabiner* used by German fire fighters. They were introduced in the Eastern Alps around 1910. The Stettner boys learned about carabiners while climbing in the German and Austrian Alps. Several people have claimed that Joe and Paul were likely the first to use these carabiners in America. See *Rock & Ice*, No. 79, Knapp, Fred, "Stroke of Genius: The History of American Rock Climbing," May/June 1997, pp. 44-56. Professor Albert Ellingwood and Barton Hoag had used pitons on Lizard Head in 1920, but there is no evidence that they used carabiners.

9. Rock climbing shoes of this type are discussed by Karl Lukan in his book *The Alps And Alpinism*, plate 88.

10. Upon Joe's death, Jack Fralick published a short version of "The

Stettner Way"in *Climbing* (No. 169, June 15-August 1, 1997, p. 48). His original article appeared in Vol. XXX, No. 1, of the *Chicago Mountaineer*, a journal for Chicago Mountaineering Club members. The title of this story was taken from this article.

11. Hersey was a well-known British solo-climber living in Boulder who was killed while soloing a route in Yosemite.

12. Actually the year was 1941, four years later.

13. Fralick is the one who brought the confusion about the Stettner and Beckey couloirs to the attention of Leigh Ortenburger, author of *A Climber's Guide To The Teton Range.* Ortenburger then borrowed films of the Stettners' 1941 climb from Paul Stettner and showed them to Grand Teton National Park rangers. The rangers studied the films and concluded that the climb Joe and Paul did was indeed the "Beckey Couloir."

14. Bill Plumley (William J.) wrote colorfully about this trip in an article entitled "Mountain Madness," published in the *Chicago Mountaineer*, Winter 1998, #3, pp. 4 - 22.

15. Except for the famous Mummery Crack on the Grepon, a name that was bestowed by others.

16. Joe and Paul had obtained this rope from Fritz Wiessner.

17. To put matters in some perspective, Dave Roberts in his article "The 'Gunks' are a rock climber's dream of a cliffscape paradise," *Smithsonian*, August 1996, p.32, calls Fritz Wiessner "one of the greatest mountaineers in history."

18. Ormes was very impressed with the climb. Shortly afterwards, he wrote an article for the *American Alpine Journal,* Vol. 5, 1943-1945, pp. 76-80, entitled "Longs Peak," in which he described all the technical rock routes on the mountain. He wrote, "The most stimulating route is the Stettner . . . Every rock climb has a character of its own which is far more than a matter of length and difficulty. There are treacherous climbs, easy climbs, gay romping climbs, quiet climbs, versatile climbs, simple astonishing climbs. The Stettner is hard, sunny and exacting — the rock climber's route on a rock climber's peak."

19. Bill wrote a technical article about his experiences for the American Meteorogical Society. See Plumley, William, "Winds Over Japan," *Bulletin of the American Meteorological Society* 1994.

20. See generally Besser, Gretchen, "Minnie Musters The Mob," in *Ski Magazine*, March 1983.

21. Coquoz, Rene, *The Invisible Men On Skis: The Construction Of Camp Hale And The Occupation By The 10th Mountain Division, 1942-45.*

22. In 2001 Earl Clark was elected to the Colorado Ski Hall of Fame for his life long commitment to skiing and, in particular, to the Tenth Mountain Division. Earl enlisted in the Army in 1942 as a private, was assigned to the first battalion of the 87th Infantry because of his experience and love for the mountains, became a "six month wonder," and returned to the 87th as a second lieutenant. He accompanied the 87th Infantry to Italy, engaged in the campaign there and was a captain at the end of the war. Remaining in the Army reserves, he retired as a lieutenant colonel. In 1971, Earl became the first president of the National Association of the Tenth Mountain Division (1971).

23. Earle, George, *History of the 87th Mountain Infantry, Italy, 1945.*

24. Remarks of Col. David M. Fowler, Commander, 87th Mountain Infantry Regiment

25. The award of the Silver Star to Paul was reported in the *Chicago Mountaineering Club Newsletter*, Vol. I, No. 2, April to August 1945. Anne apparently placed little significance on the award at the time.

26. Edith Riedl was born in Budapest, Hungry, on April 28, 1911. She died in Chicago on August 9, 1995.

27. Seph and Pepi were common German nicknames for Joseph. Others often referred to Joe by both of these names. His father's [Joseph Sr.] nickname was Seph. Edith usually called Joe "Pepi"; other relatives called him "Sepp."

28. Six months after this discussion, Joe's wish for me was fulfilled. I met Laura Luc, whom Joe liked a lot. They partied together, corresponded and spoke on the telephone. Eight months after Joe's death, we were married.

29. As best as can be ascertained, this statement is accurate. Paul, however, allowed his son Paul Jr., to lead on the 50th Anniversary attempt on the Stettner Ledges.

30. Joe was actually seven years older than Paul Petzoldt.

31. In October of 1941 Petzoldt joined Ernest Field and Warren Gorrell from Rocky Mountain National Park in an attempt to rescue Charles Hopkins, who had parachuted to the top of Devils Tower and was unable to get down. Petzoldt failed to lead completely the Durrance Crack rescue, but succeeded as part of the rescue team led by Jack Durrance himself.

32. This statement about being circus performers is, to use a term from Petzoldt's title, a "tale," in this case one that is devoid of any literal truth. On the other hand, if he was simply engaging in hyperbole to make a point about the "Stagners" climbing abilities, he was likely on the mark.

33. Forty-three years later, when located and invited to attend the CMC"s golden anniversary celebration in 1990, Bill expressed great surprise that the Club still existed. Harold, at the time, was gravely ill and on June 15, 1990, crossed over the "Great Divide," as older mountaineers sometimes put it. Bill followed him on January 17, 1996. Their ashes lie scattered at the base of their beloved Tetons.

34. Five years later, Walter March was elected President of the Chicago Mountaineering Club. See *CMC Newsletter*, Vol. IX, No. 1, 1955. He served in that capacity for two years.

35. It wasn't quite that simple, as Joe explained in Chapter 15. According to Joe, Ebert had selected Paul Petzoldt to lead, but Joe said, "If I don't lead, I don't climb." In any event, it seems that John Ebert was happy with his final choice.

36. Vol. III. No. 3, 1950; reprinted in the *Chicago Mountaineer*, Sept. 1977.

37. This film has been transferred to VHS video tape, a copy of which may be obtained from the Chicago Mountaineering Club.

38. As always, this is a serious issue in mountaineering. Although the courts hold that there is no legal duty to undertake another's rescue, the ethical side of this age-old dilemma is unresolved. For example, see the passages on this issue in

Jon Krakauer's *Into Thin Air* (1997), ch. 18; and the report in *Accidents in North American Mountaineering 2000*, p. 27-28, about eight McKinley climbers who were unwilling to help solo climber Shigeo Tamoi. Tamoi had collapsed at the 19,500-foot level and was in a semi-conscious state. Slovak climber Michal Krissak, also soloing McKinley, took considerable risks in rescuing Tamoi. This is not the place to debate this complex issue. However, from what follows, there can be little doubt about Joe Stettner's position on this issue.

   39. Published in *CMC Newsletter*, Vol. XI, No. 5, October 1957, pp. 10-12. The incident occurred in August 1957. In a letter found in Joe's effects, Joe referred to this incident as a "so-called 'rescue incident.'" Letter of Joe Stettner of September 21, 1957. Modesty aside, the so-called "rescue incident" did establish a new route on Lefroy.

   40. Years later, Ruth and John Mendenhall wrote *Introduction to Rock & Mountain Climbing,* Stackpole Books (1969).

   41. In the early 1950s, Joe fashioned a couple of metal tubes to be used as a summit registry upon which was engraved "In Memory of John Speck, Chicago Mountaineering Club." One of these was placed on the summit of Sharkstooth, a spectacular peak in Rocky Mountain National Park, Colorado.

   42. Anne Stettner informed me that Paul was not on the Warbonnet climb and that Bollinger was leading this climb. The *Chicago Mountaineering Club Newsletter,* Vol., No. 6, Dec. 1995, pp. 23-25, confirms this. According to this report, Karl Bollinger was leading a climb of Warbonnet with Gaurang Yodh and Tom Nathan. Bollinger had crossed over a ridge out of sight of his belayer Yodh, apparently fell about 30 feet and was knocked unconscious. He was wearing a European-style chest harness (attached only to his chest and not his waist) and, while unconscious, may have simply slipped out of his harness and fell a thousand feet to his death. Paul was the group outing chairman and led the rescue party the next day. They found Gaurang and Nathan in good shape. Bollinger was found on a snow field below.

   43. Whether Joe was "lucky and got away with some things" depends upon one's perspective. In July 1952, Joe took a serious fall at Devils Lake. He was lucky in the sense that he wasn't more seriously injured, but only in that sense. A couple of times, Joe mentioned to me that he had taken a fall and hurt his back but did not elaborate. I found Joe's report of the incident, made for the Chicago Mountaineering Club Newsletter, Vol. VI, No. 3, September 1952.

> "It happened to me as it can happen to any one of us rock climbers. Here I was flat on my back, my feet close to the edge of a thirty-five foot drop, gasping for air -- uh . . . , if you know what I mean. Blood was running down over my face, my left ear was badly chopped up, and my back hurt very much. I could hear loud yells for help from my and other nearby climbing parties. Jay Orear was holding me until I slowly sat up and assured him that I was not interested in going farther; the 20-25 foot bounce was enough for me. After feeling my bones for possible breaks, I lay back and thought the whole thing over.

"Oh yes, Aletta Kramer, Payton Courtney, and Jay & Jeanne Orear were climbing with me on the west bluff of Devils Lake. After lunch Aletta left us, but the rest of us wanted a bit more workout around Turks Head. As usual, I stressed the importance of using rope on our practices; still, on this last climb I did not have a rope on myself. I was demonstrating a hand traverse, a very nice little climb about ten feet above a ledge, about three feet wide. The feet are merely used against the wall for friction as one leans out and goes hand over hand along a solid slab about 4 - 5 inches think which, after a length of ten feet or so, thins out and leads to the ledge below a crack. The firm handhold gave me a secure feeling and I leaned out, which in turn gave a good footing on the vertical wall. We had climbed this place several times before, but this time my luck gave way; or should I say the rock gave way? As this happened Courtney was standing just below me. Since he was not watching as a good boy should, I fell with my back on his left shoulder, somersaulting backward; and I was on my way for a 25 ft. tumble to the next ledge. On the way I picked on a couple of medium sized trees that slowed me down enough to bring me to a halt.

"After my breath came back and I had some rest, I walked down to the car and Bobby Palser gave me a ride to Baraboo for first aid and X-rays to check my aching back.

"So this is my story; there may be other variations of it. The date was July 5th; and the night of the 6th was a very long one for me and perhaps for others too around me. By this time I am all right; that is, as good as I was before the accident."

44. This statement is not entirely true. According to Jack Fralick, he, Joe and Paul got together for a climb at Devils Lake in 1969. Paul tried a move but discovered he couldn't do it. "It used to be that if I could get my fingers on it, I could climb it," Paul lamented.

45. Paul Jr., had not planned on letting the senior contingent lead any of the pitches. Thus, it would be the first of their serious climbs that neither Joe nor Paul would lead. The plan was to have three climbing teams ("ropes") of two climbers.

46. This is not an accurate statement. The first rope team of Paul Jr., and Herb Keishold managed to reach Broadway, the end of the Stettner Ledges climb. They arrived in a hail storm. Paul Jr. reported that "Dad was over half way up, but it was too late to continue, so we decided to turn back. Dad was doing well. I came down and bivouacked with Dad. It was rain, hail and lightning that stopped us. It was not a matter of just not making it. In any case, we had a fine time." It also was not true that anyone got sick, according to Paul Jr.

significant climbs

"All my climbs were made without guides, and most of them in the company of my brother Paul. He is almost five years younger, and he did a large part of the leading on our most important climbs."

— Joe Stettner

Joe on Lone Eagle Peak, 1933.

Jack Fralick assisted in the compilation and elaboration of the Stettners' list of significant climbs. Fralick has remarked several times that, "as far as we know, neither Joe nor Paul ever climbed as a second on the rope to anyone other than each other."

Joe and Paul's climbs

1920 — Dreitorspitze (Wetterstein Mountains, Germany)
1921 — Stubaier Mountains (Austria)
1922 — Zugspitze (Germany) in winter and summer;
         Wiesbachhorn, Bratschenkoepfe, Glocknerin,
         Grossglockner, Gross-Venediger (Joe's narrative
         indicates summit not reached), Totenkirchl
         (Wilde Kaiser) (all in Austria)
1923 — Totenkirchl (Austria); Gross-Venediger on skis (Austria);
         Zugspitze, Dreitorspitze, Staffelstein and
         Kampenwand (all in Germany);
         Tretach, Madelgabel, Wolfebenerspitze,
         Hochvogel (all in Germany)
1924 — Geierspitze on skis (Lizumer Mountains, Austria);
         Scheffauers (Austria), Tretach (Germany)
1925 — Alpspitze, Nebelhorn (Germany); Schaufelspitze,
         Zuckerhuedl, Stubaier-Wildspitze (all in Austria)
1927 — Rocky Mountain National Park (RMNP), Colorado,
         new route on East Face of Longs Peak known as
         "Stettner Ledges"

1928 — Glacier Park, Montana, Mt. Rockwell, Garden Wall, Blackfeet Mountain.

1930 — RMNP, Colorado, Longs Peak by Alexanders Chimney (Paul and Anne)

1931 — RMNP, Colorado, Longs Peak by Alexanders Chimney (Joe and Fannie); Navajo and Apache Peaks

1932 — Indian Peaks, Colorado, Mts. Toll and Shoshoni, Navajo and Apache Peaks (Joe)

1933 — Colorado, Lindberg Peak [Lone Eagle Peak], North Face by new route; RMNP, Longs Peak, North Face by new route; Navajo and Apache Peaks

1936 — RMNP, Colorado, Longs Peak, East Face by new route [Joe's Solo]; by North Wall, right of regular route; Little Matterhorn; Navajo and Apache Peaks

1937 — Grand Teton National Park (GTNP), Wyoming, Grand Teton by North Ridge (fourth ascent); Mt. Owen by regular route with first ascent of direct variation; Middle Teton by Dike Route, a new variation

1939 — Crestone and Milwaukee Peaks, Sangre de Cristo Range, Colorado

1941 — GTNP, Wyoming, Mt. Owen, Teewinot, Mt. St. John and Symmetry Spire by regular routes, Rock of Ages by new route on the North Face (Paul suffered a 30-foot leader fall); Grand Teton, first ascent of incorrectly named Beckey Couloir (their route of descent from the North Ridge in 1937)

From 1942 onward, Joe's climbs without Paul, except for 1946 and Devils Tower in 1949

1942 — Colorado, Indian Peaks area, Apache and Navajo Peaks; RMNP, Longs Peak by Alexanders Chimney and by Stettner Ledges, third ascent (Joe led, with Bob Ormes)

1945 — Acted as chief guide for Iowa Mountaineers on its outing to the Tetons. Climbed Grand Teton, Middle Teton, South Teton and Teewinot by regular routes and Nez Perce by new route on upper South Face of East Summit (Joe led, with John Speck) (films of many of these climbs available through the Chicago Mountaineering Club)

1946 — Wind River Mountains, Wyoming, Gannett Peak by Gooseneck route and south ridge; Pinnacle Ridge, Woodrow Wilson and Bastion.

1947 — Needle Mountains, San Juan Range, Colorado, Sunlight, Eolus, Glacier Point, Jagged Mountain, Needle Ridge

by new route; Monitor by new route (East Face), and
North Thumb by possibly new route (Joe led, with
Edith and Jack Fralick)

1948 — Acted as chief guide for the Iowa Mountaineers on
their outing to the Wind River Mountains, Wyoming,
climbed Gannett Peak, Ramparts, Bastion, Sacagawea,
Fremont, Dinwoody and Mt. Koven; Devils Tower,
Wyoming, by Durrance Crack (Joe, eighth ascent)

1949 — Devils Tower, Wyoming, by Durrance Crack, Joe led
the first rope of the Chicago Mountaineering Club;
Paul led the second rope (eleventh ascent)

Paul's climbs without Joe

1930 — RMNP, Colorado, Alexanders Chimney (with Anne,
engagement climb)

1936 — GTNP, Wyoming, Grand Teton, Petzoldt-Loomis
Otter Body route (second ascent, first descent; with Art
Lehnebach)

1949 — Big Horn Mountains, Wyoming, Black Tooth, West
Ridge, new route (with Chicago Mountaineering Club
party); Hallelujah, North Corner, new route
(with Jack Fralick and Al Philipp)

1951 — RMNP, Colorado, traverse of Chiefs Head and Pagoda
(with Jack Fralick)

1960 — Canadian Rockies, Mt. Temple, Eiffel, Pyramid,
Snow Dome (with Anne & Jack Fralick)

19?? — Wind River Range, Pingora

1977 — RMNP, Colorado, Stettner Ledges (50th Anniversary attempt,
Paul Stettner Jr. led, with Al Johnson, Gordon and Molly
Brown, and Herb Keishold)

Joe rappeling off
Mt. Owen after
new route in 1937.

Joe placing protection.

A Glimpse of Military Life

Here are several glimpses at life in the famed Tenth Mountain Division, including an outline of the mountaineering school training schedule in Joe's 87th Mountain Infantry, an equipment list for the ski trooper and the typical menu.

Joe's 87th Mtn. Inf. Mountaineering School Training Schedule

MORNING 1ST DAY

CLIMBING PACE & AIDS

  A — Save Energy

    1. Moderate but steady pace.

    2. Length of steps vary with the terrain.

    3. Rhythmical breathing.

    4. Proper selection of route.

    5. Not too long or too frequent halts.

    6. Short lift of foot uphill.

    7. Swing around obstacles rather than over them.

    8. The "rest step" is valuable on steep slopes and at high altitudes.

    9. Place the sole of the boot flat on the ground.

    10. Climb steep slopes in zig-zags.

ELEMENTARY ROPE TECHNIQUE

  A — Knots.

    1. Middlemens or Butterfly.

     2. Overhand.

     3. Bowline.

     4. Bowline on a bight.

     5. French bowline.

     6. Square knot.

B — Distance between men.

C — Belays

     1. Ice axe.

     2. Ice pitons.

     3. Body.

     4. Natural (ice hummocks).

     5. Rock.

     6. Rock pitons.

D — Care and Handling of the Rope.

     1. Rope discipline.

     2. Carrying and storage of climbing rope.

E —Use of Rope and Ice Axe.

     1. Anchor loop.

     2. Hand loop.

     3. Hand coils.

AFTERNOON 1ST DAY

ICE TECHNIQUE

A — Use of Crampons. (The sole of the boot must always be
    parallel to the slope.)

     1. Traversing.

     2. Climbing up slopes of varying degree.

B — Step Cutting.

     1. Use of axe.

     2. Step to be flat and sloping inward.

     3. Steps at zig-zag corner.

     4. Steps in descending.

C — Arrests.

     1. Alone.

     2. Anchor man.

D — Roped Party Ascents and Descents.

SNOW TECHNIQUE

A — Step kicking.

B — Traversing Uphill.

C — Glissading.

D — Descents.

     1. With crampons.

     2. Heeling down.

E — Arrests.

MORNING 2ND DAY

AVALANCHE FACTORS

  A — Factors.

      1. Incline of slope.

      2. Inner structure.

      3. Shape.

      4. Temperature.

      5. Wind.

      6. Depth of snow.

      7. Ground cover.

      8. Recent and past weather.

      9. Prior avalanches.

      10. Knowledge of country above.

  B — Types.

      1. Wind slab.

      2. Dry.

      3. Wet.

RESCUE TECHNIQUE

  A — Avalanche Rescue.

      1. Estimation of distance victim moved after last seen.

      2. Probing and digging patterns.

  B — Crevasse Rescue.

      1. Bilgeri method.

      2. Prusik knot.

AFTERNOON 2ND DAY

ELEMENTARY ROCK TECHNIQUE

  (REMEMBER: The rope is for your safety and is not a tow rope.

  If in doubt — rope up. Don't wait and experiment in dangerous spots.)

  A — Route Planning.

      1. Constantly plan ahead.

  B — Climbing Essentials. — Demonstration.

      1. Body vertical to slope.

      2. Three point suspension.

      3. Proper use of hand and footholds.

      4. Climb with the legs and feet — avoid use of arms and hands.

      5. Correct use of the rope.

  C — Practice Footholds and Handholds near Ground — Unroped.

  D — Belays.

      1. Natural (rock projections).

      2. Body - Shoulder - Hip - Knee.

      3. Piton.

Tenth Mountain Division troops engaging in training to evacuate injured personnel near Camp Hale. Joe had this scheduled on the fifth day. (Courtesy U. S. Army)

MORNING 3RD DAY

ELEMENTARY ROCK TECHNIQUE
1. Roped climbing and descending on comparative difficult routes.   (Single).
2. Rappelling for beginners.
3. Stopping short falls.

AFTERNOON 3RD DAY

RAPPELLING & ADVANCED CLIMBING
1. Rappelling.
2. Roped in partys (piton belays).
3. Rappelling (advanced). Methods of retrieving rope.
4. Roped partys — piton belays.
5. Stopping short falls.

MORNING 4TH DAY

ADVANCED ROCK TECHNIQUE
1. Crack climbing — will not admit body.
2. Chimney climbing — will admit body.
3. Rib climbing.
4. Advanced rappelling.

AFTERNOON 4TH DAY

ROCK PITON TECHNIQUE
1. When used.
2. How used.
   a. Method of driving.
3. Practice in driving (vertical — lateral).
4. Roped parties using pitons.

MORNING 5TH DAY

ADVANCED ROPE AND ROCK TECHNIQUE
1. Rope tension climbing.
2. Overhangs.
3. Roped party climbing.
4. Tyrolean Traverse.

AFTERNOON 5TH DAY

MOUNTAIN FREIGHTING TECHNIQUE
1. Moving weapons and equipment up cliffs by means of ropes.
2. Handling of injured personnel.
3. Placing of fixed ropes.

Tenth Mountain Division cartoons.

Equipment List for a Ski Trooper

3 sets summer underwear
2 sets winter underwear
3 pairs O.D. [olive drab] socks
3 pairs light wool socks
3 pairs ski socks
3 pairs heavy wool stockings

2 pairs brown shoes, dress
1 pair ski boots
1 pair rubber overshoes
1 pair rubberbottom shoes
1 pair mountain climbing shoes (nailed)
2 pair of innersoles

2 pairs of O.D. trousers, dress
2 pairs of suntain trousers, dress
1 pair skitrousers
1 pair white trousers (camouflage)
1 pair work trousers (fatigue)
2 wool O.D. shirts, dress
2 suntain shirts

1 comb, 1 toothbrush
1 cake of soap
1 safety razor and blades
1 shavingbrush
1 pair identification tags (dogtags)

1 Soldiers Fieldmanual

2 overseas, suntain caps
1 O.D. cap
1 workhat (fatigue)
1 skicap, 1 reversible parka
1 overcoat, 1 raincoat
1 O.D. blouse (dress), 1 field jacket
2 work jackets (fatigue)
1 pair wool gloves
4 handkerchiefs, 1 bath & 2 face towels
2 ties suntain, 1 tie black
1 pair wool mittens
1 pair canvas mittens (shells)
1 framepack (rucksack)
2 barracksbags
1 messkit, knife fork & spoon
1 kanteen, 1 pocketknife, (skirepair)

1 pair skis complete
    with poles (all Northland)
1 pair climbers (skins)
1 pair snowglasses
1 pair gaiters
1 pair leggings
1 wool sweater long sleeves
1 rubber foodbag
1 metal skitip

Typical Menu MT – 3
Breakfast

Peaches, Cereal and Milk, Biscuits and Butter, Coffee

Dinner

Peaches, Cheese, Biscuits, Chocolate Candy, Lemonade

Supper

Soup, Canned Luncheon Meat, Rice, Biscuits and Butter, Hard Candy, Tea

Glossary of climbing Terms

Placing a piton. (Courtesy Colorado Mountain Club)

Artificial or direct aid: A method of climbing in which the climber uses the protection, e.g. piton, for a handhold or foothold.

Belay, to belay, belayer: Originally a nautical term, meaning to fasten; in climbing it means to secure the climber. The lead climber sets up a secure place on the climb or a "belay" (noun), from which the "belayer" (the non-climber at this point) feeds out or takes in the climbing rope for the purpose of minimizing the length and severity of a fall by the climber. In doing this, the "belayer" "belays" (verb) the climber. Usually when the climber reaches his goal or climbs the total length of the climbing rope, he sets up a "belay" for the "belayer," who then becomes the climber. Through this leap frog method, a climbing team is able to climb, stage by stage, a rockwall in relative safety.

Carabiner: A metal snap link used by climbers to attach a climbing rope to the protection the lead climber places in the rockwall during a climb.

Chimney, chimneying: A wide crack large enough for the climber to get inside. Chimneying is technique developed for climbing chimneys. The climber puts his back against one side of the wall and his feet against the other side, forming a bridge. By bending and straightening the legs, it is possible to climb or walk up the chimney.

Crampons: Metal, tooth-like grips a climber attaches to his climbing boots to make footing secure and safe during a snow or ice climb.

Piton: A metal spike with a hole at one end through which a carabiner is placed. Pitons are pounded into cracks of a rock wall for protection.

Protection: Rope slings, pitons, metal nuts, etc., placed in a rock wall by the lead climber. The second climber will later remove this protection. Protection is used with the aid of a carabiner to connect the climbers rope and thereby reduce the length or severity of a fall.

Stemming or bridging: A climbing technique in which the climber straddles a gap to form a bridge. He places one leg on one side and the other leg on the other.

Traverse: Climbing sideways or horizontally.

*Joe on the Grande
Teton in the 1930s.*

A

B

C

P

R

S